ROYAL COURT

Royal Court Theatre presents

BLACK MILK

by **Vassily Sigarev**

First performance at the Royal Court Jerwood Theatre Upstairs
Sloane Square, London on 31 January 2003.

Black Milk is produced as a Genesis Project with additional support from the British Council.

BLACK MILK

by **Vassily Sigarev**

Cast in order of appearance

Poppet **Sarah Cattle**
Levchik **Paul Ready**
Ticket Clerk **Suzan Sylvester**
Mishanya **Gary Oliver**
Auntie Pasha **Di Botcher**
Petrovna **Sheila Reid**
Drunk **Alan Williams**

Director **Simon Usher**
Designer **Delia Peel**
Lighting Designer **Simon Bennison**
Sound Designer **Ian Dickinson**
Casting **Lisa Makin, Amy Ball**
Production Manager **Sue Bird**
Stage Managers **Vicki Liles, Helena Lane Smith**
Stage Management Work Placement **Emily Peake**
Costume Supervisor **Iona Kenrick**
Company Voice Work **Patsy Rodenburg**

The Royal Court Theatre would like to thank the following for their help with this production: Wardrobe care by Persil and Comfort courtesy of Lever Fabergé.

THE COMPANY

Vassily Sigarev (writer)
For the Royal Court: Plasticine.
Other plays include: The Vampire's Family, The Lie
Detector, The Russian Lottery, Ladybird Ladybird.
Awards include: Evening Standard's Charles
Wintour Award 2002 for Most Promising
Playwright, Anti-Booker Prize (Plasticine 2000),
Debut Prize (Plasticine 2000), Eureka Prize (Black
Milk 2002). Vassily has been part of the Russian
'New Writing' Group which has worked with the
Royal Court since 1999.

Simon Bennison
Theatre includes: The Price (Tricycle Theatre); The
Contractor, Comedians, Troilus & Cressida (Oxford
Stage Company); Yard, Howie the Rookie
(Revived), Normal (Bush Theatre).
Dance includes: Sophie, Stateless, Between
Shadows, Unstrung Tension, Three Unspoken
Words, Traces (Cathy Marston/Royal Ballet),
Pointless (George Piper Dances/Roundhouse), Sea
of Troubles (Macmillan/Adam Cooper revival),
Palimpset (Shobana Jeyasingh), Tick, Last Night of
the Empire (Tom Sapsford), Closer, On the Bone
(Emma Diamond), Renard (Royal Ballet).
Opera includes: Carmen (English Touring Opera).
He also lit the Samsung Pavilion at the Sydney 2000
Olympics, and has been a member of the Royal
Opera House lighting department since 1991.

Di Botcher
Theatre includes: Beauty and the Beast (Dominion);
Cats (New London); Cardiff East, Sunday in the
Park with George, A Little Night Music, Under Milk
Wood, The Absence of War, Sweeney Todd (RNT);
Kes, The Frogs (RNT Studio); A Midsummer
Night's Dream, Speculators, Lady Audley's Secret,
Richard III (RSC); Card Boys (Bush); Flesh and
Blood (Hampstead); The Oyster Catchers
(Swansea); Into the Woods (Manchester); Moll
Flanders (Colchester); Small Change (Haymarket,
Basingstoke).
Television includes: Cruise of the Gods, Belonging
(series three and four), 'Orrible, People Like Us,
Fun at the Funeral Parlour, Light in the City, Alistair
McGowan's Big Impression, Sunburn, Rhinoceros,
Kavanagh QC, The Silent Twins, The Bill, District
Nurse, Harpur and Iles, The Armando Ianucci
Show, Casualty, Tipping the Velvet, High Hopes.
Film includes: Twin Town, All or Nothing, Life and
Debt.
Radio includes: An Easy Game to Play, Lord of
Misrule, A Bizarre Sort of Child, Night People,
Imperial Palace.

Sarah Cattle
For the Royal Court: Made of Stone,
Naturalised.
Other theatre includes: Inside Out (Clean
Break); Boeing, Boeing (Lyceum, Crewe);
Peril at End House (Grand, Wolverhampton);
American Days (Mill Studio, Guildford); A
Midsummer Night's Dream (Chilworth
Manor).
Television includes: Rockface, Linda Green,
Film includes: Silent Cry, Hans Christian
Anderson.

Ian Dickinson (sound designer)
For the Royal Court:
Crazyblackmuthafuckin'self, Caryl Churchill
Season, Imprint, Mother Teresa is Dead, Push
Up, Workers Writes, Fucking Games, Herons,
Cutting Through the Carnival.
Other theatre includes: Port (Royal Exchange
Manchester); Night of the Soul (RSC
Barbican); Eyes of the Kappa (Gate); Crime
and Punishment in Dalston (Arcola Theatre);
Search and Destroy (New End, Hampstead);
Phaedra, Three Sisters, The Shaughraun,
Writer's Cramp (Royal Lyceum, Edinburgh);
The Whore's Dream (RSC Fringe, Edinburgh);
As You Like It, An Experienced Woman Gives
Advice, Present Laughter, The Philadelphia
Story, Wolks World, Poor Superman, Martin
Yesterday, Fast Food, Coyote Ugly, Prizenight
(Royal Exchange, Manchester); Great
Monsters of Western Street (Throat Theatre
Company); Small Craft Warnings, Tieble and
Her Demon (Manchester Evening News
Theatre Awards Best Design Team), The
Merchant of Venice, Death and The Maiden
(Library Theatre Company, Manchester).
Ian is Head of Sound at the Royal Court.

Sasha Dugdale
Sasha has translated several Russian plays for
the Royal Court, including How I Ate a Dog
by Evgeny Grishkovets, Vassily Sigarev's
Plasticine and Terrorism by the Presnyakov
Brothers.

Gary Oliver

Theatre includes: A Streetcar Named Desire, Sing Yer Heart Out for the Lads, The Cherry Orchard (RNT); Angels in America (Library Theatre); Squash, Then What (Old Red Lion); Comedy of Errors (RSC tour/Young Vic); Unidentified Human Remains (Royal Exchange); Salvation (Gate); The Fire Raisers, The Slow Approach of Night (Arts Threshold); The Lizzie Play (Theatre Clwyd & tour); Look Back in Anger, King Lear, Endgame (Wink Productions); Romeo & Juliet (Factotum Touring Company); Shoemaker's Wonderful Wife (BAC/Ragazzi Theatre Company); Puppet Play of Don Christabel (Ragazzi Theatre Company); The Importance of Being Earnest (Stephen Joseph Theatre).

Television includes: The Bill, Kavanagh QC, Casualty, Heartbeat, Soldier Soldier, Eastenders, Rules of Engagement, Discoveries of the World.

Film includes: Horizontal Man.

Delia Peel

As designer theatre includes: Old Vic New Voices (Old Vic); Dona Rosita the Spinster, Comedy of Errors (Oval House Theatre); I Am Angela Brazil, The Advertisement, Musicians Crossing a Bridge without Their Instruments (Auden Theatre, Norfolk); Cabaret, The Importance of Being Earnest (Oxford Playhouse); The Rise and Fall of Little Voice, Travels with My Aunt, Duet for One (Theatre Royal, Bury St Edmunds); West Side Story (Spier Summer Festival, Stellenbosch, South Africa); The Wild Duck, The Pillars of the Community (Oxford School of Drama); Monkey in the Middle (Tristan Bates Theatre).

As assistant designer: Luther (RNT).

Opera includes: Aventure and Nouvelle Aventure (Quays Theatre, The Lowry Centre, Salford), Carmen (Spier Summer Festival, Stellenbosch, South Africa/Wilton's Music Hall).

Designed and devised Don't Tell Porky Pies (Tristan Bates Theatre).

Education work includes: The Brodsky Quartet Song Project, Share Music, Edinburgh/Pembroke, Wales.

Paul Ready

For the Royal Court: Crazyblackmuthafuckin'self.

Theatre includes: Romeo & Juliet (Liverpool Playhouse); Mother Clap's Molly House (RNT/Aldwych); Twelfth Night (Liverpool Playhouse/Everyman); Cuckoos (Gate/RNT Studio); The Beggar's Opera (Broomhill Opera/ Wilton's Music Hall).

Television includes: Jeffrey Archer: The Truth, Heartbeat, Tipping the Velvet, Chambers, Harry Enfield Presents, Princess of Thieves, Poirot, Plain Jane, The Practice.

Film includes: Maybe Baby, Angels & Insects.

Sheila Reid

For the Royal Court: The Gentle Avalanche, Small Change, My Mother Said I Never Should.

Theatre includes: The Good Hope, Sweeney Todd, Caritas, Three Sisters, Hedda Gabler, The Crucible, Love's Labours Lost, Othello, The Beaux Stratagem (RNT); Tartuffe, The Wood Demon, Lear, Ruling The Roost (The Actors Company); Cousin Vladimir, Romeo & Juliet, 'Tis Pity She's a Whore, King Baby (RSC); When I Was a Girl I Used to Scream and Shout (Whitehall/Bush); The Marshalling Yard, One Flea Spare (Bush); Façades, Crime and Punishment (Lyric); The Winter Guest (West Yorkshire Playhouse/ Almeida); Martin Guerre (Prince Charles); Steaming (Piccadilly); Misalliance (Chichester); The Importance of Being Earnest (Chichester/Haymarket)Snake in the Grass (Peter Hall Company/Old Vic); Separate Tables, Up in the Eighties (Kings Head); Into the Woods (Donmar); The Circle (Oxford Stage Company); Abandonment (Traverse);The Actress and the Bishop, If I'm Glad You'll Be Frank (Young Vic).

Television includes: Flickers, Get Lost, The Emmigrants, Taggart, Dr Finlay, Oliver's Travels, The Cruel Train, Ghostbusters of East Finchley, My Wonderful Life, Where the Heart Is, The Sleeper, Monarch of the Glen, Midsomer Murders, The Bill.

Film includes: The Touch, Brazil, American Friends, Sir Henry at Rawlinson's End, Othello, Five Days One Summer, The Winter Guest, Watch That Man, Still Crazy, Felicia's Journey, Mrs Caldicot's Cabbage War.

Radio includes: The House, Colville & Soames, Villette.

Sheila also wrote her own shows Terrible With Raisons In It and Love Among the Butterflies (London/Edinburgh/Stratford-upon-Avon).

Suzan Sylvester

For the Royal Court: Cleansed.

Other theatre includes: The Real Thing (tour); The Secret Rapture (Minerva, Chichester); Betrayal (Northcott, Exeter); Shang-a-Lang (tour); Card Boys (Bush); Terms of Abuse (Hampstead); The Reckless are Dying Out (Lyric); The House of Bernada Alba (Theatr Clwyd); Yiddish Trojan Women, Kindertransport (Cockpit); Three Sisters (Chichester); Love's Labour's Lost (Royal Exchange); Life is a Dream (West Yorkshire Playhouse); All My Sons, , Romeo and Juliet (Young Vic); The Glass Menagerie (Young Vic/tour); An Enemy of the People (Young Vic/Playhouse); As You Like It, The Seagull, The Government Inspector (Crucible); Pericles, All's Well That Ends Well (RSC); 'Tis Pity She's a Whore, A Small Family Business, Tons of Money (RNT); A View from the Bridge (RNT/Aldwych).

Television includes: The Bill, Doctors, Casualty, Where the Heart Is, Maisie Raine, Touch of Frost, London's Burning, Holding On, Wycliffe, Pie in the Sky, Casualty, Peak Practice, Rides, Mysterioso, Call Me Mister.

Film includes: Streets of Yesterday.

Radio includes: Pentecost, Macbeth, The Last Dare, The Rover.

Awards include: Laurence Olivier Award for Most Promising Newcomer for A View from the Bridge.

Simon Usher (director)

For the Royal Court: Mother Teresa is Dead, Herons.

Other theatre includes: Sing Yer Heart Out For the Lads (RNT); Musicians Crossing a Bridge Without Their Instruments (Dial Theatre); Looking at You (Revived) Again, The Evil Doers, Pond Life, Not Fade Away, The Mortal Ash, All of You Mine, Wishbones, Card Boys (Bush); King Baby (RSC, Pit); The War in Heaven, Timon of Athens, Pericles, The Winter's Tale, The Broken Heart, The Lover's Melancholy, French Without Tears, The Bells, Pale Performer, Trios, Lettice and Lovage, The Naked, Murders in the Rue Morgue (Haymarket, Leicester); Waiting for Godot, The Browning Version, Heartbreak House, Hamlet, Les Liaisons Dangereuses, Whole Lotta Shakin' (Belgrade, Coventry); No Man's Land (English Touring Theatre); Mr Puntila and His Man Matti (Chichester); Can't Stand Up for Falling Down (Watford Palace and tour); Burning Everest, Exquisite Sister (West Yorkshire Playhouse); The Wolves (Paines Plough); Twins (Birmingham Rep); Great Balls of Fire (Cambridge Theatre, West End).

Alan Williams

For the Royal Court: Crave (Paines Plough and Bright Ltd tour), Local, Bed of Roses, Weekend After Next (Hull Truck tour).

Other theatre includes: The Inland Sea (Oxford Stage Company); The Sea (Chichester Festival); The Jew of Malta (Almeida & tour); The Rib Cage, To the Chicago Abyss (Manchester Royal Exchange); Kiss the Sky (Bush); Vigil (Arts Club Theatre, Vancouver); The Darling Family (Theatre Passe Muraille, Toronto); White Dogs of Texas (Taragon Theatre, Toronto & tour); The Cockroach Trilogy (Hull Truck tour UK/US/Canada); Having a Ball (Liverpool Playhouse); Mean Streaks (Hull Truck tour/Bush); Small Ads (King's Head); Mary Barnes (Birmingham Rep); Prejudice, Eejits (Liverpool Everyman); Bridget's House (Hull Truck tour).

Television includes: Peterloo, Serious and Organised, Paradise Heights, Wire in the Blood, Sirens, The Bill, Peak Practice, Coronation Street, The Mayor of Casterbridge, Love in a Cold Climate, Badger, Always & Everyone, Touching Evil, Getting Hurt, The Scold's Bridle, Wycliffe.

Film includes: Bright Young Things, Heartlands, All Or Nothing, Elephant Juice, Among Giants, The Cockroach that Ate Cincinnati, Coleslaw, The Darling Family, Daughters of the Country.

Radio includes: Five Letters Home to Elizabeth.

THE ENGLISH STAGE COMPANY AT THE ROYAL COURT

The English Stage Company at the Royal Court opened in 1956 as a subsidised theatre producing new British plays, international plays and some classical revivals.

The first artistic director George Devine aimed to create a writers' theatre, 'a place where the dramatist is acknowledged as the fundamental creative force in the theatre and where the play is more important than the actors, the director, the designer'. The urgent need was to find a contemporary style in which the play, the acting, direction and design are all combined. He believed that 'the battle will be a long one to continue to create the right conditions for writers to work in'.

Devine aimed to discover 'hard-hitting, uncompromising writers whose plays are stimulating, provocative and exciting'. The Royal Court production of John Osborne's Look Back in Anger in May 1956 is now seen as the decisive starting point of modern British drama and the policy created a new generation of British playwrights. The first wave included John Osborne, Arnold Wesker, John Arden, Ann Jellicoe, N F Simpson and Edward Bond. Early seasons included new international plays by Bertolt Brecht, Eugène Ionesco, Samuel Beckett, Jean-Paul Sartre and Marguerite Duras.

The theatre started with the 400-seat proscenium arch Theatre Downstairs, and then in 1969 opened a second theatre, the studio Theatre Upstairs. It frequently transfers productions to the West End, such as Caryl Churchill's Far Away, Conor McPherson's The Weir, Kevin Elyot's Mouth to Mouth and My Night With Reg and also co-produces plays, such as Sebastian Barry's The Steward of Christendom and Mark Ravenhill's Shopping and Fucking (with Out of Joint), Martin McDonagh's The Beauty Queen Of Leenane (with Druid Theatre Company), Ayub Khan-Din's East is East (with Tamasha Theatre Company, and now a feature film).

Since 1994 the Royal Court's artistic policy has again been vigorously directed to finding and producing a new generation of playwrights. The writers include Joe Penhall, Rebecca Prichard, Michael Wynne, Nick Grosso, Judy Upton, Meredith Oakes, Sarah Kane, Anthony Neilson, Judith Johnson, James Stock, Jez Butterworth, Marina Carr, Phyllis Nagy, Simon Block, Martin McDonagh, Mark Ravenhill, Ayub Khan-Din, Tamantha Hammerschlag, Jess Walters, Che Walker, Conor McPherson, Simon Stephens, Richard Bean, Roy Williams, Gary Mitchell, Mick Mahoney, Rebecca Gilman, Christopher Shinn,

Kia Corthron, David Gieselmann, Marius von Mayenburg, David Eldridge, Leo Butler, Zinnie Harris, Grae Cleugh, Roland Schimmelpfennig, Vassily Sigarev and DeObia Oparei. This expanded programme of new plays has been made possible through the support of A.S.K Theater Projects, the Jerwood Charitable Foundation, the Genesis Foundation, the American Friends of the Royal Court Theatre and many in association with the Royal National Theatre Studio and the British Council.

In recent years there have been record-breaking productions at the box office, with capacity houses for Caryl Churchill's A Number, Jez Butterworth's The Night Heron, Rebecca Gilman's Boy Gets Girl, Kevin Elyot's Mouth To Mouth, David Hare's My Zinc Bed and Conor McPherson's The Weir, which transferred to the West End in October 1998 and ran for nearly two years at the Duke of York's Theatre.

The newly refurbished theatre in Sloane Square opened in February 2000, with a policy still inspired by George Devine.

INTERNATIONAL PLAYWRIGHTS

Since 1992 the Royal Court has placed a renewed emphasis on the development of international work and a creative dialogue now exists with Cuba, Brazil, France, Germany, India, Palestine, Russia, Spain, Uganda and the United States. Many of these projects are supported by the British Council and the Genesis Foundation.

The Royal Court's exchange with Russian new writing began in 1999and since then the Royal Court has led a number of workshops in Moscow, Novosibirsk and Ykaterinburg. Vassily Sigarev took part in this play development work. Extracts from one of the projects developed in Russia, Moscow Open City, were performed as part of the International Playwrights Season 2000. In May 2001 the Royal Court presented a week of rehearsed readings New Plays from Russia. In March 2002 Plasticine was produced as part of the International Playwrights Season.

The International Playwrights: FOCUS RUSSIA is produced by the Royal Court International Department:
Associate Director **Elyse Dodgson**
International Administrator **Ushi Bagga**
International Associate **Ramin Gray**

AWARDS FOR
THE ROYAL COURT

Jez Butterworth won the 1995 George Devine Award, the Writers' Guild New Writer of the Year Award, the Evening Standard Award for Most Promising Playwright and the Olivier Award for Best Comedy for Mojo.

The Royal Court was the overall winner of the 1995 Prudential Award for the Arts for creativity, excellence, innovation and accessibility. The Royal Court Theatre Upstairs won the 1995 Peter Brook Empty Space Award for innovation and excellence in theatre.

Michael Wynne won the 1996 Meyer-Whitworth Award for The Knocky. Martin McDonagh won the 1996 George Devine Award, the 1996 Writers' Guild Best Fringe Play Award, the 1996 Critics' Circle Award and the 1996 Evening Standard Award for Most Promising Playwright for The Beauty Queen of Leenane. Marina Carr won the 19th Susan Smith Blackburn Prize (1996/7) for Portia Coughlan. Conor McPherson won the 1997 George Devine Award, the 1997 Critics' Circle Award and the 1997 Evening Standard Award for Most Promising Playwright for The Weir. Ayub Khan-Din won the 1997 Writers' Guild Awards for Best West End Play and Writers' Guild Best New Writer of the Year and the 1996 John Whiting Award for East is East (co-production with Tamasha).

At the 1998 Tony Awards, Martin McDonagh's The Beauty Queen of Leenane (co-production with Druid Theatre Company) won four awards including Garry Hynes for Best Director and was nominated for a further two. Eugene Ionesco's The Chairs (co-production with Theatre de Complicite) was nominated for six Tony awards. David Hare won the 1998 Time Out Live Award for Outstanding Achievement and six awards in New York including the Drama League, Drama Desk and New York Critics Circle Award for Via Dolorosa. Sarah Kane won the 1998 Arts Foundation Fellowship in Playwriting. Rebecca Prichard won the 1998 Critics' Circle Award for Most Promising Playwright for Yard Gal (co-production with Clean Break).
Conor McPherson won the 1999 Olivier Award for Best New Play for The Weir. The Royal Court won the 1999 ITI Award for Excellence in International Theatre. Sarah Kane's Cleansed was judged Best Foreign Language Play in 1999 by Theater Heute in Germany. Gary Mitchell won the 1999 Pearson Best Play Award for Trust. Rebecca Gilman was joint winner of the 1999 George Devine Award and won the 1999 Evening Standard Award for Most Promising Playwright for The Glory of Living.

In 1999, the Royal Court won the European

theatre prize New Theatrical Realities, presented at Taormina Arte in Sicily, for its efforts in recent years in discovering and producing the work of young British dramatists.

Roy Williams and Gary Mitchell were joint winners of the George Devine Award 2000 for Most Promising Playwright for Lift Off and The Force of Change respectively. At the Barclays Theatre Awards 2000 presented by the TMA, Richard Wilson won the Best Director Award for David Gieselmann's Mr Kolpert and Jeremy Herbert won the Best Designer Award for Sarah Kane's 4.48 Psychosis. Gary Mitchell won the Evening Standard's Charles Wintour Award 2000 for Most Promising Playwright for The Force of Change. Stephen Jeffreys' I Just Stopped by to See The Man won an AT&T: On Stage Award 2000.

David Eldridge's Under the Blue Sky won the Time Out Live Award 2001 for Best New Play in the West End. Leo Butler won the George Devine Award 2001 for Most Promising Playwright for Redundant. Roy Williams won the Evening Standard's Charles Wintour Award 2001 for Most Promising Playwright for Clubland. Grae Cleugh won the 2001 Olivier Award for Most Promising Playwright for Fucking Games. Richard Bean was joint winner of the George Devine Award 2002 for Most Promising Playwright for Under the Whaleback. Caryl Churchill won the 2002 Evening Standard Award for Best New Play for A Number. Vassily Sigarev won the 2002 Evening Standard Charles Wintour Award for Most Promising Playwright for Plasticine. Ian MacNeil won the 2002 Evening Standard Award for Best Design for A Number and Plasticine.

ROYAL COURT BOOKSHOP

The bookshop offers a wide range of playtexts and theatre books, with over 1,000 titles. Located in the downstairs Bar and Food area, the bookshop is open Monday to Saturday, afternoons and evenings.

Many Royal Court playtexts are available for just £2 including works by Harold Pinter, Caryl Churchill, Rebecca Gilman, Martin Crimp, Sarah Kane, Conor McPherson, Ayub Khan-Din, Timberlake Wertenbaker and Roy Williams.

For information on titles and special events, Email: bookshop@royalcourttheatre.com
Tel: 020 7565 5024

REBUILDING THE ROYAL COURT

In 1995, the Royal Court was awarded a National Lottery grant through the Arts Council of England, to pay for three quarters of a £26m project to completely rebuild its 100-year old home. The rules of the award required the Royal Court to raise £7.6m in partnership funding. The building has been completed thanks to the generous support of those listed below.

We are particularly grateful for the contributions of over 5,700 audience members.

English Stage Company Registered Charity number 231242.

THE AMERICAN FRIENDS OF THE ROYAL COURT THEATRE

AFRCT support the mission of the Royal Court and are primarily focused on raising funds to enable the theatre to produce new work by emerging American writers. Since this not-for-profit organisation was founded in 1997, AFRCT has contributed to nine productions They have also supported the participation of young artists in the Royal Court's acclaimed International Residency.

If you would like to support the ongoing work of the Royal Court, please contact the Development Department on 020 7565 5050.

Funded by
THE
ARTS
COUNCIL
OF ENGLAND

PROGRAMME SUPPORTERS

The Royal Court (English Stage Company Ltd) receives its principal funding from London Arts. It is also supported financially by a wide range of private companies and public bodies and earns the remainder of its income from the box office and its own trading activities.

The Royal Borough of Kensington & Chelsea gives an annual grant to the Royal Court Young Writers' Programme and the Affiliation of London Government provides project funding for a number of play development initiatives.

The Jerwood Charitable Foundation continues to support new plays by new playwrights through the Jerwood New Playwrights series. Since 1993 the A.S.K. Theater Projects of Los Angeles has funded a Playwrights' Programme at the theatre. Bloomberg Mondays, the Royal Court's reduced price ticket scheme, is supported by Bloomberg. Over the past seven years the BBC has supported the Gerald Chapman Fund for directors.

TRUSTS AND FOUNDATIONS
American Friends of the Royal Court Theatre
A.S.K Theater Projects
The Carnegie United Kingdom Trust
Carlton Television Trust
Gerald Chapman Fund
The Foundation for Sport and the Arts
Genesis Foundation
The Goldsmiths' Company
The Haberdashers' Company
Paul Hamlyn Foundation
Jerwood Charitable Foundation
John Lyon's Charity
The Mercers' Company
The Laura Pels Foundation
Quercus Charitable Trust
The Peggy Ramsay Foundation
The Eva & Hans K Rausing Trust
The Royal Victoria Hall Foundation
The Peter Jay Sharp Foundation
The Sobell Foundation
The Trusthouse Charitable Foundation
Garfield Weston Foundation
Worshipful Company of Information Technologists

MAJOR SPONSORS
American Airlines
BBC
Bloomberg
Channel Four
Lever Fabergé
Royal College of Psychiatrists

BUSINESS MEMBERS
Aviva plc
BP
Lazard
McCann-Erickson
Pemberton Greenish
Peter Jones
Redwood
Siemens
Simons Muirhead & Burton

MEDIA MEMBERS
Beatwax
Columbia Tristar Films (UK)
Hat Trick Productions

PRODUCTION SYNDICATE
Anonymous
Jonathan & Sindy Caplan
Kay Hartenstein Saatchi
Richard & Susan Hayden
Kadee Robbins
William & Hilary Russell

INDIVIDUAL MEMBERS
Patrons
Anonymous
Advanpress
Mrs Alan Campbell-Johnson
Ms Kay Ellen Consolver
Coppard and Co.
Mrs Philip Donald
Robyn Durie
Tom & Simone Fenton
Homevale Ltd
Mr & Mrs Jack Keenan
New Penny Productions Ltd
Caroline Quentin
Ian & Carol Sellars
Jan & Michael Topham
Amanda Vail

Benefactors
Martha Allfrey
Anonymous
Jeremy & Amanda Attard-Manché
Matilde Attolico
Emma Bleasdale
Jasper Boersma
Brian Boylan
Katie Bradford
Julian Brookstone
Yven-Wei Chew
Lucy Bryn Davies
Ossi & Paul Burger
Debbi & Richard Burston
Danielle Byrne
Martin Cliff
Peter Czernin
David Day
Winston & Jean Fletcher
Joachim Fleury
Charlotte & Nick Fraser
Judy & Frank Grace

Sue & Don Guiney
Amanda Howard Associates Ltd
Peter & Maria Kellner
Lee & Thompson
Colette & Peter Levy
Ann Lewis
Christopher Marcus
David Marks
Barbara Minto
Eva Monley
Paul Oppenheimer
Janet & Michael Orr
Maria Peacock
Jeremy Priestley
Simon Rebbechi
John & Rosemarie Reynolds
Kate Richardson
Samuel French Ltd
Nicholas Selmes
Jenny Sheridan
Peregrine Simon
Brian D Smith
John Soderquist
The Spotlight
Anthony Wigram
Thai Ping Wong
George & Moira Yip
Georgia Zaris

Associates
Anonymous
Eleanor Bowen
Mrs Elly Brook JP
Mrs Helena Butler
Carole & Neville Conrad
Margaret Cowper
Barry Cox
Andrew Cryer
Zoë Dominic
Jacqueline & Jonathan Gestetner
Michael Goddard
Phil Hobbs - LTRC
Tarek J Kaseem
Carole A. Leng
Lady Lever
Mr Watcyn Lewis
Christopher Marcus
Nicola McFarland
Mr & Mrs Roderick A McManigal

Pat Morton
Gavin & Ann Neath
Georgia Oetker
Lyndy Payne
Pauline Pinder
William Poeton CBE &
Barbara Poeton
John Ritchie
Bernard Shapero
Kathleen Shiach
Lois Sieff OBE
John Soderquist
The Spotlight
Sue Stapely
Peter & Prilla Stott
Carl & Martha Tack
Will Turner
Anthony Wigram
Thai Ping Wong
George & Moira Yip
Georgia Zaris

STAGE HANDS CIRCLE
Graham Billing
Andrew Cryer
Lindy Fletcher
Susan & Richard Hayden
Mr R Hopkins
Philip Hughes Trust
Dr A V Jones
Roger Jospe
Miss A Lind-Smith
Mr J Mills
Nevin Charitable Trust
Janet & Michael Orr
Jeremy Priestley
Ann Scurfield
Brian Smith
Harry Streets
Thai Ping Wong
Richard Wilson OBE
C C Wright

Association of
London Government   LONDON ARTS

FOR THE ROYAL COURT

BLACK MILK

Vassily Sigarev

2

Characters

NARRATOR

'POPPET', *or* SHURA, *twenty-five*

LYOVCHIK, *twenty-eight*

TICKET CLERK, *forty-five*

MISHANYA, *thirty-five*

AUNTIE PASHA LAVRENYOVA, *fifty*

PETROVNA, *seventy*

DRUNKEN MAN

CROWD, *carrying toasters*

Notes

Russian names have been transcribed in order to give a sense of their sound and not according to official systems of transcription.

Poppet and Lyovchik first appear in Act One as MAN *and* WOMAN, *while in Act Two Pasha Lavrenyova first appears as* WOMAN,

ACT ONE

NARRATOR. Where should I start? I don't know . . . with the name of the town, maybe? Well, it's not exactly a town. Not even a largish village. Definitely not a village. In fact, it's not really even a populated place. It's a station. Just a station. Somewhere in the middle of My Boundless Motherland. But when I say middle, I don't mean at the heart. Because My Boundless Motherland is a strange animal and its heart, as everyone knows, is located in its head. But enough of that. The head, I mean. We should work out exactly where we are. I reckon that it's about in the region of the small of the back, the sacrum, or maybe even . . . No, no 'maybe' about it – that's where it is. That's where we are. Right in the centre of it. The epicentre. Things are all painfully out of step here . . . Things are really not right. In fact, so wrong that I want to scream, wail, yell, just so My Boundless Motherland will hear, 'You slut . . . You're not decent!' But would she hear? Would she understand? Stop to think about it? I don't know . . .

But this station is called Mokhovoye. As usual the name isn't written on the board. And why should it be? None of the trains even stop here. Only the freight-passenger trains. The expresses, the private trains and all the other ones rush through without dropping their speed, and even sometimes speeding up so as not to catch an accidental glimpse of anything untoward. Anything 'like that', if you know what I mean. Not even all the local trains stop here. The 6.37 and the 22.41 Eastbound and the 9.13 Westbound and that's it. That is it . . .

The station is a wooden building with a slate roof, standing next to the railway track. It's November and cold. There is snow on the platform. There's a path through the snow leading right to the station doors. It's not as cold in there. You might even call it quite warm.

Shall we go in? Warm up?

We go in. Looks alright, actually. Hardly a disgrace. The walls were painted not so long ago. Three years or so, no more. The paint's dark green, but that's a matter of taste, as they say . . . Enough of them, anyway . . . the walls, I mean. What else have we got here? Somewhere to sit? There is. Two lots of station seats right in the middle. In one of the seats, closest to the iron stove, which is like a column, built into the wall, there's a man asleep. His head is thrown back and his mouth is open wide. He's a little man, frail, but for all that he's clearly a bit the worse for wear. He's asleep. Let him sleep. We'll leave him be for the moment. Let's have a look round to begin with. Right. Next to the stove is a pile of logs, a heap of rubbish and some papers or other. Going further, there's a word scratched into the wall (but a harmless one, thank God) and a plywood board with the timetable stencilled on it: Arrivals, departures, waiting time at station (minutes). In the column 'waiting time at station' there are little number ones going all the way down. Well, that's logical – if you're not here, you've missed it. Anyway . . . what else? Hey! Left luggage lockers. Six of them. Out of order and filthy dirty. Shame . . . we could have . . . then there's a metal door, a new one, unpainted. A metre from the door there's a window with a grille over it – the ticket office. A piece of paper is stuck to the window. It reads 'All gone', yet what is all gone, why and when is not clear. But it isn't our business anyway. A woman is sitting behind the window. The ticket clerk. She's a nice, firm forty-five and she's wearing the lining from a Chinese leather coat and felt boots. Her face is smeared with a French (made in Poland) beauty mask. She is holding some knitting in her hands and she has an expression of utter boredom in her eyes.

Silence.

Only the man gives out indistinct noises from time to time and there is the clicking of the knitting needles in the clerk's hands. But nothing else. It is as if it's a painted scene and not a real one.

But no . . .

Can you hear? Some voices. They're coming closer. Closer. Still closer.

Who's this?

We're about to find out.

The door opens. A MAN *and a* WOMAN *appear. They are both young, sleek, lightly dressed. They are holding armfuls of checked canvas laundry bags – about three in each hand. And on top of all this the* WOMAN *is pregnant.*

WOMAN (*city accent*). What a place. I almost went into labour. Why the hell did we get out at this hole.

MAN (*city accent*). S'alright – we've made ourselves a tidy sum.

WOMAN (*putting bags down*). How can they live here? It's a filthy pit. Ugh! Did you see what their nails are like?

MAN (*putting bags down*). Y'what?

WOMAN. Their nails . . . You wouldn't see that, not even in the Hermitage. Like black peoples', their nails . . . You see them?

MAN. For the love of . . . No, I didn't see them.

WOMAN (*looking at the seat*). Do you reckon it's safe to sit down?

MAN. Why the hell not?

WOMAN. Might catch something. Bacteria. Gangrene. TB. (*She pats her tummy.*) Not recommended, apparently. I can't have any injections or antibiotics.

MAN. Put down some newspaper and you can sit there as long as you like.

WOMAN. Hey! That's an idea. Which one?

MAN. The furthest one.

The WOMAN *goes into her bag, gets out a pile of papers and spreads them out on two seats next to each other for her and the* MAN. *She sits down and sniffs.*

WOMAN. It smells of armpits in here a bit. Remember that old guy on the train?

MAN (*studying the timetable, indifferent*). Which one?

WOMAN. With a beard and that. Can't remember.

MAN. And?

WOMAN. The smell he was giving off. Jesus . . .

MAN. What?

WOMAN. I mean I took a sniff and phwoar . . . Started taking every second breath . . . Thought I was going to die. Gas chamber, it was . . . What the fucking hell are we doing in this shithole? You've really done . . .

MAN. We've not done badly out of this, alright.

WOMAN. What's that mean?

MAN. Not bad.

WOMAN. Is it a fucking secret?

MAN. Would shifting five bags suit you?

WOMAN. Fucking hell. Not bad.

MAN. Well then.

Silence.

WOMAN. Shit, it stinks of armpits in here. What a nuisance. Fuck.

She gets out a bottle of perfume and without looking sprays all around herself. Her hand lands on the DRUNKEN MAN*'s open mouth. She looks – her eyes almost fall out of her head – she screeches, jumps up and runs outside.*

MAN. What's wrong with you, Poppet? (*Looks at the man.*) What the . . . What are you doing here? (*Goes over.*) Oi! . . . you still alive? (*He nudges the old man with his foot.*) What you going around scaring people for? Eh! Do you want a toaster? It's free. Hey, have you snuffed it? Eh, you going to take this toaster or what?

POPPET (*opening the door a crack and looking in carefully*).
   Lyovchik, who is it?

LYOVCHIK. Some old bloke.

POPPET. Is he dead?

LYOVCHIK. Pissed.

POPPET. What?

LYOVCHIK. Pissed.

POPPET. Old git! Almost gave birth 'cause of him. He's
   settled in nicely, hasn't he?

LYOVCHIK. Weren't you looking?

POPPET. No, I wasn't looking. I only sat down. It's not like
   I haven't got things to worry about, without having to look
   out for shit everywhere. What's he doing here anyway?

LYOVCHIK. Sleeping, isn't he.

POPPET. He can go home and sleep.

LYOVCHIK. Tell him then.

POPPET. You tell him yourself. Like I need it. He bit me as
   well, the bastard!

LYOVCHIK. What with?

POPPET. His mouth.

LYOVCHIK. He hasn't got any teeth. And never had, I reckon.

POPPET. What do you mean?

LYOVCHIK. Just that. Have a look.

POPPET. You serious? (*She approaches.*)

LYOVCHIK. Have a look, go on.

POPPET (*holds her nose and looks in the man's mouth*). He
   hasn't! Where are they?

LYOVCHIK. Drunk his way through them.

POPPET. No. Really?

LYOVCHIK. He's probably got some disease . . .

POPPET. Yuk! I could catch something! (*She wipes her hand with a handkerchief.*)

LYOVCHIK. Forget it. It's already taken hold.

POPPET. What?

LYOVCHIK. Soon your teeth will start falling out and all.

POPPET. Oh, piss off, you stupid git. (*Turns away.*) What the fuck are we doing in this hole? This is a right pain in the arse.

LYOVCHIK (*creeps up behind her and jabs her in the small of the back with his index finger*). Ahhh!

POPPET (*jumps and squeals*). Have you fucking lost your mind! I could go into labour right now . . . And you see what sort of baby I'll give you: a spastic . . . a clown . . .

LYOVCHIK. Hey, Poppet . . . I didn't mean it . . . it was only . . . y'know . . . a sign of love . . .

POPPET. A sign of love . . . You're that fucking idiot from Dostoyevsky, you are. (*Pause.*) Go and get the tickets and we can get out of here. This place is winding me up. Give me a fag.

LYOVCHIK (*gets out the packet*). Is smoking allowed here, do you reckon?

POPPET. It is for pregnant women. (*Takes a cigarette. Lights up and smokes with affected elegance.*) Will you stop standing around like a Jewish mountaineer in the plains of Mongolia and go and get the fucking tickets.

LYOVCHIK. Are you in a strop then, Poppet?

POPPET. That's right.

LYOVCHIK. You've got a spot by your nose, Poppet.

POPPET. Very funny. Don't wet yourself laughing . . . Where? (*She gets out a little mirror and looks in it.*) It's all these infections round here – I've caught something. Where?

LYOVCHIK. Joke.

POPPET. Piss off, you useless bastard, I've had it up to here with you.

LYOVCHIK. What you getting so uptight about?

POPPET. Nothing.

LYOVCHIK. Well that's alright then.

POPPET. Yeah.

LYOVCHIK. Yeah.

POPPET. That's alright then. (*She sits down on the windowsill and turns towards the window, smoking.*)

LYOVCHIK *stands there a bit longer and then goes over to the ticket window. The* CLERK *doesn't look at him.*

LYOVCHIK. Madam . . . (*The* CLERK *doesn't answer.*) Excuse me, madam . . .

CLERK. What d'you want?

LYOVCHIK. Unit Trading, the leaders in the Russian household appliances market, have chosen you to be the lucky recipient of a super-prize . . .

CLERK (*jumps up, rubbing the mask off her face*). Bugger off!

LYOVCHIK (*not even faltering*). I don't think you've understood me, madam. Unit Trading, leaders in the Russian household appliances market, have chosen you to be the recipient of a super-prize, an invaluable kitchen helpmate – the wonder toaster from Kanzai, a leading manufacturer of household goods and audio and video equipment.

CLERK. Bugger off . . .

LYOVCHIK. This wonder toaster has the following amazing advantages: the body of the toaster is made of high-density ecological super-plastic, making it super-long-lasting and unbreakable. The wonder toaster's element is made from a unique super-combination of nickel and chrome, allowing you to save between three and six times the electricity. This wonder toaster is simple to use, needs no servicing and has a super contemporary design. It will save you valuable time, make you super-toast, giving you an energy burst lasting the whole day, and will generally become your best friend and a member of your family. If you are interested in this offer and you are not yet the proud owner of a wonder toaster, Unit Trading will give you this one as a present. And if you aren't interested in the offer for some reason, or you already have your own wonder toaster, we suggest you order a catalogue from our company. Our internet address is www.ru.

Pause.

CLERK. You finished pouring out your soul? Go on then, sod off.

LYOVCHIK. You've got me wrong, madam.

CLERK. For a start, I'm not a madam. Miss.

LYOVCHIK. You've got me wrong, miss.

CLERK. And for a second start, I'm a trader myself with a bit of experience and your patter won't work on me. Understand?

POPPET. Lyovchik, you tell her to piss off. She's taking liberties.

CLERK (*sticks head out of window*). You can keep quiet, you silly little cow. And if you're going to smoke go outside. Smoking away in here . . .

POPPET (*without looking at the* CLERK). Get lost.

CLERK. What?

POPPET. You heard. Take a long walk to . . . Macau.

CLERK (*mishears*). Who did you call a cow, you little prat?

POPPET. I'm looking at her.

LYOVCHIK. So miss, are you interested in our offer?

CLERK. Move away from the window, you prat. You're
   stopping me working.

LYOVCHIK. What a shame you've chosen not to take the
   unique opportunity of becoming the proud owner of a
   wonder toaster.

CLERK. Get on with you. I've already got a couple.

LYOVCHIK (*leaves the window and goes across to* POPPET).
   What you doing, frightening off the customers?

POPPET. What customers? That old battleaxe? She'll sell it
   back to you and buy it for a cut-down price . . . I want a
   Chupa.

LYOVCHIK. You can want all you like.

POPPET. Oh, fuck off. (*Pause.*) Have you got one then?

LYOVCHIK. I've got everything.

POPPET. Then give me one.

LYOVCHIK. Pretty please.

POPPET. Oh, piss off. (*Pause.*) Why you being such a tight
   bastard?

LYOVCHIK. There you go. (*Gets out a Chupa Chups lolly.*)
   Stuff yourself.

POPPET (*grabs the Chupa Chups, unwraps it and sticks it in
   her mouth*). You get stuffed. Let's get out of here. It's
   winding me up here. Bloody fleapit. Nowhere to get pissed.

LYOVCHIK. What you mean, nowhere? Bloke over there's
   had a few and he isn't getting in anyone's way.

POPPET. What are you suggesting? I should do the same?

LYOVCHIK. Well? You were the one who brought the bump along into battle.

POPPET. Piss off. They're probably knocking back the local homemade potato-brew round here.

CLERK (*sticking head out of the window*). No home-brew here!

LYOVCHIK. Oh, miss! Miss, have you had a think about becoming a proud owner of the wonder toaster?

CLERK. Well, go on then, show us what you've got and I'll have a look.

LYOVCHIK (*reaching into bag*). It's said you shouldn't look a gift horse in the mouth.

CLERK. Round here we look first.

LYOVCHIK. Who's we?

CLERK. We in the trade.

LYOVCHIK. Ooh. Nice. And what do you trade, if it's not a secret?

CLERK. It's a secret.

LYOVCHIK. State secret, is that? (*Gets out a toaster in its box.*)

CLERK. Nearly. (*She disappears back into the hatch.*)

Sound of a bolt sliding back. The iron door opens and the CLERK *comes out into the hall.*

Go on then, show us what you've got.

LYOVCHIK (*gets out the toaster and shows it to her*). Invaluable kitchen helpmate, wonder toaster from Kanzai, the leading manufacturers of household appliances and also audio and video equipment.

CLERK (*looking the toaster up and down with a sceptical glance*). You telling fibs to an old woman? This is what you cook bread in. My cousin has one of these.

POPPET. That's exactly what it is.

CLERK. Who asked you? Come on, give it here. (*She takes the toaster and turns it around, looking at it.*) Made in China?

LYOVCHIK. Come off it, miss. This is made in Malaysia.

CLERK. What are you on about? I can see it's made in China. You haven't got any winter boots?

LYOVCHIK. 'Fraid not.

CLERK. Shame. I'd have taken the boots. I'm in these felt ones. No gloves?

LYOVCHIK. Only toasters.

CLERK. I'd have taken the gloves, too. But only kid gloves. 'Cause I had some, but I left them on the train. I'm not local myself, see. I just work here. I come over on the train. Been doing it for two years. I've just learnt how to make vodka. I brew it up at home and then bring it down here to sell. Quite good quality actually. Keeps the locals happy. No one's been poisoned yet. Touch wood. Course, the useless bastards drink like it's going out of fashion. The demand, as they say, is outrunning the supply. Where do they put it all? But I mean if you think about it, what else is there to do round here? No cinema, no TVs . . . They can't get good reception round here – 'cause it's in a dip. So they drink. And that's a good thing. I've come into a little bit of money at last. Bought myself a divider, an unpolished one. Unpolished is all the rage now. Walnut coloured. Not bad. Bit special. What else did I buy? Two coats from the Chinese and the Turks and a fridge. With one of those . . . what's it called . . . with two doors. There was something else. Oh yeah, I had some decorating done. I'm not going to leave here now for anything. I'll work right through to my pension. And I'll keep going then, if they let me. Just now I need a downright fortune – Got to marry off my daughter. My daughter's called Varka, Varvara. Like Yakubovich's girl. I like the look of him, my goodness, that Yakubovich. Ooh, I could really go for him . . . (*Whispers.*) I'll tell you a secret – I'm going to be on that game show 'Wheel of

Fortune'. That's between us, right . . . Anyway Varka's my
daughter and I need to get her married off straightaway,
she's twenty-five already and never been under a bloke.
Horror to look at. Unbelievably ugly. And the main thing
is she's getting uglier all the time. Spots everywhere. About
seventy on each cheek. Obvious why she's got them. Not
sexually mature . . . They'll go as soon as she starts living a
full life. But to get her started, I need some money. To hook
some bloke or other. And then I'll have to slip him more to
keep him there. So I'll be here until I'm pensioned off. Still,
a cosy spot for it.

LYOVCHIK. Well you need the toaster then. You make him
toast every morning and he'll never leave.

CLERK. Just the thing. How much are you asking?

LYOVCHIK. Absolutely free of charge.

CLERK. You're having me on. Free. You can't even use the
toilet for free anymore.

LYOVCHIK. Absolutely free of charge. You just pay delivery.

CLERK. How much?

LYOVCHIK. A mere two hundred roubles.

CLERK. What?! Did it travel in a separate compartment?
Hundred and fifty.

LYOVCHIK. Two hundred, lady. A gift horse . . .

CLERK. We look it in the mouth round here. Hundred and
fifty.

LYOVCHIK. Two hundred. For delivery.

CLERK. Hundred and seventy. That's my limit.

POPPET. Come on – that thing cost five hundred.

CLERK. Who asked you. Hundred and seventy. 'Cause it's
made in China.

LYOVCHIK. Malaysia.

CLERK. China. Can't fool me. Hundred and eighty.

LYOVCHIK. Malaysia. It's yours.

CLERK. For a hundred and seventy.

LYOVCHIK. Hundred and eighty.

CLERK. But we agreed on a hundred and seventy, didn't we?

LYOVCHIK. No we didn't.

CLERK. Did.

LYOVCHIK. Didn't. Go on. Take it.

CLERK. Hundred and seventy?

LYOVCHIK. Hundred and seventy. A hundred and seventy.

CLERK. Yes! I love bargaining with men, oooh I do. When
I go on this 'Wheel of Fortune', if I get a prize out of them,
well I'll do some bargaining then. Whole country will
remember, the bargaining I'll do. Being a trader is a calling,
not a job to me. I'm the trader of traders, I am. Don't need
to tell you – just look at how my business has grown. The
sign there, that means that I'm out of vodka. There's one of
my usuals snoring over there. Look at him and my heart is
content. You must be kidding, I wouldn't leave this place for
anything. I'll leave here in a box and that's the only way.
A cosy corner. As long as they don't all die on me. 'Cause
recently they've been dropping like overbred dogs. Dying
out, once and for all. I won't have any customers soon. I've
got competition now as well.

LYOVCHIK. Serious?

CLERK. Small fry. Old woman passing off her home-brew
as the stuff. Early days still, but if I decide to expand the
business or she does, well we could have a conflict on our
hands.

*The door squeaks. They fall silent and look at the entrance.
The door opens a crack and an old woman's head in a
knitted scarf appears.*

Oh! Talk of the devil. What do you want, Petrovna? What you doing on someone else's patch?

PETROVNA (*comes in and stands by the door. She is holding a toaster and a bottle of home-brew vodka*). I'm . . . I'm here for them . . . I'm here to see you, my loves.

CLERK. What do you want from them? They're not going to swig your home-brew. Go on – out of here.

PETROVNA. I'm here to see you, my dears. (*She walks over slowly.*)

LYOVCHIK. What's up, love?

PETROVNA. My old man's dead, son . . .

CLERK. Ooh, liar. What old man is that, Petrovna? He was killed back in the war.

PETROVNA. My old man is dead, son. I've got nothing to bury him with.

LYOVCHIK. What's that got to do with me, dear? I'm not the social services, you know.

PETROVNA. You take this thing back and the money, mine, which I . . .

LYOVCHIK. What's wrong with you – banged your head, dearie? Had one too many?

CLERK. He's got a point, Petrovna.

LYOVCHIK. What money?

PETROVNA. Mine, which I . . .

LYOVCHIK. We haven't got your money, love. Go on. Go home. (*He turns away.*)

PETROVNA *stands there and doesn't move.*

POPPET. Go on then, old girl.

PETROVNA. My old man's dead, love. Got to bury him.

POPPET. Go on then, bury him.

LYOVCHIK. Or he'll go off.

PETROVNA. Wouldn't mind my money. And this is for you . . . (*She offers them the toaster.*) And this is, too. (*She shows them the bottle of vodka.*) A little gift, eh, love?

CLERK. What you hounding them for, Petrovna?

PETROVNA. But my old man's dead, after all . . .

CLERK. What old man? You haven't got one.

PETROVNA. I did have. And now he's died. He's lying out on the table in my room. My new old man.

CLERK. Lured someone into bed, did you?

PETROVNA. He turned up himself. Said he could help out. Helped out three days and then died.

CLERK. Whose old man was he?

PETROVNA. Mine.

CLERK. And before you, whose was he?

PETROVNA. No one's. He walked the world.

CLERK. A tramp or something?

PETROVNA. No. He was called Aleksei.

CLERK. And his surname?

PETROVNA. He couldn't remember.

CLERK. Well, Petrovna, you take the biscuit. Of all the odd things to do in your old age . . . And what do you want from them?

PETROVNA. My money. And I'll give this back to them.

CLERK. Well it's nothing to do with me. You work it out between yourselves. (*She goes over to the stove and starts throwing in firewood.*)

Silence.

PETROVNA (*looking at* LYOVCHIK). So what do you think, love?

LYOVCHIK. What do you want?

PETROVNA. I've got nothing to bury him with, eh.

LYOVCHIK. What's that got to do with me? Don't bury him then, if you haven't got the money. Take him out behind the fence and leave him there. Say you don't know who he is. What am I telling you for, anyway. You're a sensible woman. You've been around.

PETROVNA. I couldn't do that, son – it would be a sin.

LYOVCHIK. One more, one less. God will forgive you.

Pause.

PETROVNA. So how about it, love? I've got nothing at all to bury him with. Take this, why don't you. And the little gift here. And my money, which I . . .

POPPET. Lyovchik, send her packing, will you . . . she's driving me up the wall.

LYOVCHIK. What you being so difficult for? I won't take anything off you. You probably broke it, carrying it around.

PETROVNA. I haven't used it. Cross myself, I haven't used it. (*She crosses herself.*)

LYOVCHIK. That's enough, dear. Go on. Dismissed. Get off home.

PETROVNA. How can I, son, when I've got to bury the old man.

POPPET. Lyovchik, spell it out to her in four-letter words. I mean, come on . . . she's getting right up my nose.

LYOVCHIK. Did you hear that, love? They want me to send you packing. With four-letter words. Shall I go ahead, or are you going to go quietly now?

The old woman stands there without moving or answering.
Her eyes fill with tears. Suddenly she gets down on her
knees.

PETROVNA. Don't ruin me, loves. He was a kind old man.
Always pleased to see people. A wanderer. Suffered. Three
times he had frostbite in his legs, and now he's dead. Lying
on my table and we haven't washed him yet. Waiting to be
buried. And will he last? Well, that's for you to decide. How
you decide, that's how it'll be. And God will reward you
later. He will multiply your wealth. Multiply it by ten three
times, and then three times by ten. And the same for your
children and all your family for fifteen generations to come.

LYOVCHIK. Y' what? (*To* POPPET.) What's with her?

POPPET. Off her rocker, isn't she.

CLERK. She's a bit daft.

LYOVCHIK. Perhaps we should give her the money.

POPPET. Do what you like.

PETROVNA. Give it back, love, give it back.

LYOVCHIK. Alright. (*Reaches into his money belt to get out*
the money.) Listen sunshine, if God doesn't multiply my
wealth by ten three times and then three times by ten, I'll
come back and set fire to your hut.

PETROVNA. He'll multiply it by ten. By this cross, he will.

At this point the door is flung open and a procession of
people begins to move into the hall slowly: men and women
holding toasters. At the front is a strange-looking man with
a goatee. The old woman jumps up off her knees and hides
the bottle in her blouse.

VOICE IN THE CROWD. Hey, look! Petrovna's here already.
Amazing – How did you manage that, Petrovna?

PETROVNA (*looking at them from under her brow*). None of
your business.

ANOTHER VOICE. Your bloke is pissed again, Petrovna. He's built a bonfire in the yard and he's jumping around it.

PETROVNA. Let him. Nothing to do with you.

CLERK. Petrovna! Well! She's a liar, what a liar! Brilliant. We should learn from her.

General laughter. Suddenly everyone goes quiet and they look at each other.

Pause.

POPPET. Lyovchik, did you buy the tickets?

LYOVCHIK. Er . . . not yet. (*To the* CLERK.) Miss, what's-yer-name, sell us some tickets, if you wouldn't mind.

CLERK. Where you going?

FIRST WOMAN (*nudges the man with the goatee*). Mishanya, go on . . .

MISHANYA (*goes horribly pale*). Ahem . . . comrade visitors . . .

FIRST MAN. Mishka, don't be pathetic . . .

MISHANYA (*a bit less pale*). Please don't rush off, comrade visitors . . .

LYOVCHIK. How about those tickets then, miss?

CLERK. I just asked. Where are you going?

MISHANYA (*less pale still and even slightly flushed*). I am talking to you, comrade visitors.

CLERK. They want you, I reckon.

LYOVCHIK (*turning around suddenly*). Me? You talking to me? (*Advances on* MISHANYA.) Hey, you talking to me?

MISHANYA (*paling again*). You.

LYOVCHIK. Out with it then. What do you want? (*Pause.*) What's wrong? You forgotten? Off you go then. (*He turns to the* CLERK.) What you got coming up?

CLERK. Stopping service at 06.37.

LYOVCHIK (*looking at his watch*). Anything before that?

CLERK. Nothing.

POPPET. What a hole. Give us a fag, Lyovchik.

LYOVCHIK. Hang on, fuck it.

POPPET. Tight bastard.

LYOVCHIK. I said, hang on. (*To the* CLERK.) No trains then?

CLERK. Uh-huh.

LYOVCHIK. Why's the service so shit?

MISHANYA. Sir, could I just once more . . .

CLERK. For you again.

POPPET. Give us a fag, Lyovchik, go on . . .

LYOVCHIK (*gets out the packet and throws it to* POPPET).
    For fuck's sake . . . here!

POPPET. Arsehole. (*Shakes out a cigarette and puts the packet
    in her pocket.*) I'll keep them on me then.

MISHANYA. Excuse me, may I have a word?

POPPET. What you going on at him for? Can't you see he's
    having a conversation?

MISHANYA. I just wanted . . . erm . . . well . . .

POPPET. He told you to hop it. That means cut the crap and
    leave the premises. Go on. Go on.

    Pause.

    Lyovchik, you tell him, eh? You've got a way with words.

LYOVCHIK. So what you come to discuss then? I don't un . . .

MISHANYA. Well . . . it's a serious thing.

LYOVCHIK. What, exactly?

MISHANYA. I've come for justice.

LYOVCHIK. Right. Well now you're here, you'd better take it. Where is it? Not this? (*He points at the sleeping man.*)

POPPET (*laughing*). Oh Lyovchik, you're a funny bastard.

Everyone laughs except MISHANYA *and sleeping 'justice'.*

CLERK. So Mishanya, you been floored? Humour from the big city, eh? You'll be more careful in future.

FIRST WOMAN. Mishanya, get back at him . . .

FIRST MAN. Mishka, give them some brainy stuff.

SECOND MAN. Don't be pathetic, that's the main thing.

SECOND WOMAN. Look at him, he's finished.

MISHANYA (*reddening*). It's not me they're insulting, ladies and gentlemen. It's you they're insulting. All of you. One and all . . . And you just stand there. You've got nothing to say. It's a crying shame.

FIRST WOMAN. What d'you mean? We've got something to say. You've cheated us! There.

POPPET. What?

FIRST WOMAN. You cheated us.

POPPET (*advances on the woman*). Say that again, sweetheart.

FIRST WOMAN (*more subdued*). You've cheated us.

POPPET. Oh yeah?! Lyovchik, did you hear that? Did you all hear? Is that an official statement then? Are you making an official statement?

FIRST WOMAN. You what?

POPPET. This is what. You've insulted the honour and worth of our company with your words. You've compromised its prestige. We will be forced to demand compensation in the courts. Do you get me?

CLERK. Hey. That's serious. It'll be the bailiffs in next.

FIRST WOMAN (*paling*). Well, I . . . it wasn't me . . .

POPPET. Who was it then? (*To the* FIRST MAN.) Was it you?

FIRST MAN. What's it got to do with me all of a sudden? (*Hides toaster behind back.*) Actually I just came round to get vodka. Have you got any, Auntie Lusya?

CLERK. It's all gone.

POPPET (*to the* SECOND MAN). You in the cap, was it you then?

The SECOND MAN *dives into the crowd.*

Go on then. That's it. Meeting over. Back to your houses.

THIRD MAN. Got to sort this out first.

POPPET. Sort what out, darling?

THIRD MAN. We've been told that this costs fifty roubles at the market in the town.

POPPET. Have you seen them there?

THIRD MAN. No, but Mishka did.

LYOVCHIK. So what? You got them for free. So be pleased.

MISHANYA. Don't cheat us – you took money from all of us.

LYOVCHIK. Drop it, eh. Anyone got complaints about the quality? No. Excellent. Congratulations once again on becoming the proud owner of this kitchen helpmate, the wonder toaster from Kanzai. Right. Bye then. (*He sits down, gets out a Chupa Chups, unwraps it and puts it in his mouth.*)

POPPET. Lyovchik, I want one, too. (*She sits down next to him.*)

LYOVCHIK. I've already given you one.

POPPET. When? Don't lie, you bastard. You gave me a cigarette.

LYOVCHIK. And a Chupa.

POPPET. No you never. Come on, stop being a Jew.

LYOVCHIK. There you go. Just stop going on.

During this exchange the people in the crowd wave their arms, sigh and leave one by one. MISHANYA *tries to stop them. He talks. No one listens to him. They all leave. Then* MISHANYA *leaves as well. Only* PETROVNA *is left.*

CLERK. Bloody hell, they got themselves enough of your toasting machines. What in the world do they want with them. They don't even deliver bread round here. They all bake their own rolls. Honestly, the idiots. I almost feel sorry for them. Thrown away nearly half their salary on something they can't use. Now they're going to go hungry. And they've all got kids – about half a dozen each. Breeding away 'cause they're too nice or too stupid not to. Maybe they thought the state would help out. And what does the state do for them? Sod all. And then there's . . . (*Sighs.*) Live to regret it, you coming here.

LYOVCHIK. We didn't do badly here.

CLERK. Don't doubt it for a minute. Only they won't trust you again. 'Cause they always thought that (*Makes an indistinct gesture with her hand.*) up there it's all famous actors, poets and playwrights . . .

POPPET. Hey, don't go on. It's not like there's a shortage of provincial holes like this, each one with its own charms.

CLERK. Not that many, after all.

POPPET. Enough for our lifetime.

CLERK. Well, you know best, I suppose.

LYOVCHIK. Do you need the toaster?

CLERK. What for? Sooner or later one of them will exchange theirs for a bottle. They'll admire them for a month and then start finding them homes around the place. Anyway, I'm turning in. You not going home, Petrovna?

PETROVNA. I'm here . . . to see them.

CLERK. Well, do your business then . . . (*She goes back to her room.*) Come up just before the train and I'll do your tickets. (*She leaves.*)

PETROVNA. What about me, love?

LYOVCHIK. What about you?

PETROVNA. My old man did die.

LYOVCHIK. What, seriously?

PETROVNA. By this cross (*Crosses herself.*)

LYOVCHIK. Go and take a long walk.

PETROVNA. I took one the other day.

LYOVCHIK. Take another one.

POPPET. To the Hermitage.

PETROVNA. Where, love?

POPPET. The Hermitage.

PETROVNA. And what's there?

POPPET. The Hermitage (*She bursts into laughter and looks at LYOVCHIK. He isn't laughing.*) Go on, go home, eh. It's late.

PETROVNA. But what about my old man?

LYOVCHIK. That's enough, alright? Enough. You'll be dead and all soon, so why go round ruining it for everyone else?

PETROVNA (*staggers back*). Dead . . .

LYOVCHIK. Dead, yeah. What difference do these two hundred roubles make to you? You're hardly going to live to enjoy them . . .

PETROVNA. You're . . . I'm off then.

LYOVCHIK. High time.

PETROVNA. Thank you, kind people. (*She puts the toaster on the floor.*) This is for you . . . I'm off . . . (*She starts to*

*leave, then turns around and gets out a bottle from her
bosom and places it next to the toaster.*) This is for you, too.
To think of me by . . . I'm off then . . . (*She leaves.*)

POPPET. What was all that for?

LYOVCHIK. Like I care. Put it in the bag.

POPPET. Why have I got to?

LYOVCHIK. Is it difficult or something?

POPPET. Yeah, it is. My bump gets in the way.

LYOVCHIK. You and your effing bump really get on my wick.
(*He picks up the toaster and puts it in his bag.*)

POPPET. You get to me. You get right on my tits.

LYOVCHIK. Piss off.

POPPET. Piss off yourself. Prick with an arse for a head.

LYOVCHIK. Shut the fuck up, you four-legged sponger.

POPPET. Bastard. You got competition.

LYOVCHIK. And you think you haven't. You've got serious
competition.

POPPET (*flushing*). Fuck off, you prick! Understand? (*Throws
her Chupa at him.*) Wanker! (*She bursts into tears.*)

LYOVCHIK. You have a cry – won't make the competition any
less.

POPPET. Get out, I said! (*Stands up.*) Or I'm leaving.

LYOVCHIK. Shit, sit down. (*He sits her down.*) There she
goes. When we get home, you can run off where you please.

POPPET. I'll do that!

LYOVCHIK. You do it.

POPPET. I will!

*The old drunk wakes up suddenly. He gets up and looks at
them.*

DRUNK. What's going on?

POPPET (*crying*). Nothing.

DRUNK. Someone died?

LYOVCHIK. Go back to sleep. No one's died.

DRUNK. Then you should be rejoicing. But you're . . . (*He sits down again, closes his eyes and mutters.*) If no one's died you should be rejoicing. And when someone dies, then . . . 'Cause after all, life winds this way and that and it doesn't matter much which way, if someone dies . . . But people have some strange ideas . . . they're only scared of THAT SORT of death . . . and THAT SORT . . . that's nothing, that's not scary. You're gone and that's it. You gotta worry about the other sort of death. That's scary, now. 'Cause that's when your spirit dies . . . And your spirit is . . . well, that's something.

He is silent.

A train rushes through the station. There is a roaring, a clattering and everything shakes.

Silence.

LYOVCHIK *sits down next to* POPPET *and cautiously wipes away her tears with a finger.*

POPPET. When did she say the train was?

LYOVCHIK. A while yet.

POPPET. Give us a fag.

LYOVCHIK (*reaches into his pocket*). You've got them.

POPPET. Shit, I'm knackered. Like after Turkey. My back's killing me.

LYOVCHIK. It's alright. We've shifted almost five bags.

POPPET. Still got to give birth, haven't I?

LYOVCHIK. You'll be fine. It's only having a baby.

POPPET. Yeah. It's scary. (*She rests her head on* LYOVCHIK*'s shoulder.*) Let's get some sleep, eh?

LYOVCHIK. Good idea.

They close their eyes. Pause.

POPPET. Lyovchik, were you winding me up about his teeth falling out 'cause of a disease?

LYOVCHIK. Why?

POPPET. Just, my teeth feel a bit wobbly.

LYOVCHIK. I was winding you up, wasn't I?

POPPET. It's in my mind then.

LYOVCHIK. Go to sleep, eh.

POPPET. You go to sleep. (*She opens her eyes.*) Fucking issuing orders. And I threw away my Chupa 'cause of you. You're always on my back. And those nerve cells . . . they never come back, you know. Use them all up and we'll be like dummies in shop windows . . . we won't give a fuck. Already I . . .

LYOVCHIK. I said, go to sleep.

POPPET. I'm starving. My tummy's rumbling. Can you hear it?

LYOVCHIK (*shifting crossly*). Fuck's sake. You're driving me mad. Have something to eat. Who's stopping you? There's some sandwiches in the bag.

POPPET. Can't be bothered to get up.

LYOVCHIK. That's your problem.

POPPET. You could get them for your pregnant wife.

LYOVCHIK. And who'd get them for me.

POPPET. You're a real git, you are.

LYOVCHIK. I know.

POPPET. And I'm going to give birth to another one. I can see it now. I'll get sick all of a sudden and you'll be off straight away. I know your lot, you bastard. Better to die now.

LYOVCHIK (*jumps up*). For fuck's sake, cut it out! I'm sick to death of it! Just as I drop off she fucking gets going . . . Once more and you'll get a black eye, alright?

POPPET. You wouldn't.

LYOVCHIK. I would. (*Moves further away from her, sits down and closes his eyes.*)

POPPET. Off you go then. Better without you, anyway. (*She looks around and sees the bottle of vodka.*) I'm going to get fucking wasted, I am. Understand?

LYOVCHIK *doesn't reply.*

You'll have to drag me off when I've finished.

LYOVCHIK (*mutters*). Get on with it . . .

POPPET. You going to leave me here then?

LYOVCHIK *is silent.*

Right. I'm going to start drinking.

Pause.

Have we got a glass?

Pause.

Bastard.

She gets up to pick up the bottle.

Suddenly the building is rocked by a tremendous blow. The door is flung open. LYOVCHIK *jumps up from his seat.* MISHANYA *staggers in. He is disgustingly drunk. There is white at the corners of his mouth and he is carrying a double-barrelled gun.*

CLERK'S VOICE. Have you lost your mind!!! Totally . . .

MISHANYA. I'll blow you all apart!!! Bastards!!! (*He points the gun at* LYOVCHIK. LYOVCHIK *crouches down behind a seat.*) Now you're scared! (*He moves the barrel so it is pointing at* POPPET. *She pales and narrows her eyes, but doesn't move.*) Hide, you whore! I'll blow you apart!!

CLERK (*sticking head out of window*). Mikhailo, what's going on?

MISHANYA. Ahh. You destroyed this country, eh? Bastard!

CLERK. Leave off, Mishka, what you doing?

MISHANYA (*aiming at her*). Answer, when Comrade Yezhov speaks to you!

CLERK. Mishka, you've had a bit too much to drink, that's all. You're confused. It happens. It's me – Auntie Lusya.

MISHANYA. Ahhh! You! You're the one I want. Bloody well caused the genocide of the Russian people!

CLERK. By accident, Mishenka.

MISHANYA. No. It was deliberate. Ordered by the West, their Secret Services. I know everything, Pani Kaplan . . . Who shot at Lenin, eh?

CLERK. That's enough, Mishka . . .

MISHANYA. Talk! I want their names, addresses, codewords . . . who destroyed the army? Talk!

CLERK. Me, probably, I . . .

MISHANYA. Correct. So where are the pensions, the benefits, the funds? You stole them?!

CLERK. Right . . .

MISHANYA. I want bank details, account numbers . . . I'll count to three and shoot . . . Talk! One . . .

CLERK. You know what? You can go to hell!

MISHANYA. . . . two . . . talk, you counter-revolutionary!

CLERK. I'll give you counter-revolutionary in the face, I will.

MISHANYA. . . . Three.

He presses the trigger. There is a shot. POPPET *shrieks and crouches down.* LYOVCHIK *lies there, as if stuck to the floor.* MISHANYA *stands there, rocking and enveloped in smoke. The gun lies at his feet. The* CLERK *disappears. There is a second of silence, two, three seconds and then fifteen. At last the bolt is drawn back on the iron door. The* CLERK *charges out alive and well, although only wearing one boot – the other is in her hand.*

CLERK. You've done it now, you waster! You blasted hitman, you! (*She runs over to* MISHANYA *and beats him around the head with her boot.*) I'll give you shooting with a gun, I will. I'll give it to you till your barrel comes loose, I will.

MISHANYA (*covers his head with his hands*). It did it by itself, Auntie Lusya.

CLERK. I'll give you 'did it by itself'! I'll give you 'by itself' till you can't sit down for a month. (*She grabs him by the hair, bends him over and thrashes him on the buttocks with the boot.*)

MISHANYA. I won't do it again Auntie Lusya . . . I'm sorry . . .

CLERK. I can't hear anything – your popgun deafened me. (*Carries on beating him.*)

MISHANYA (*shouts*). Ow! That hurts Auntie Lusya! Ow, Auntie Lusya! Ouch!!! Auntie Lusya! (*He starts howling.*)

CLERK (*lets him go*). Get out of here!

MISHANYA (*stumbles, howling*). Thank you . . .

CLERK. Take your rifle, you stupid fool.

MISHANYA. Oh. (*He bends down to pick up the gun.*)

The CLERK *brings the boot down on his back with all her strength.* MISHANYA *starts to screech loudly, eccentrically and rushes towards the door.*

CLERK. Stop there!

MISHANYA *stops dead.*

Who got you drunk?

MISHANYA. C-c-can't remember.

CLERK. Tell Fedya if he gives you the gun once more he
won't see it again. Is that clear?

MISHANYA. Yes.

CLERK. Run along then.

MISHANYA *runs off.*

What an idiot. (*She puts on the boot.*) His brother's another
strange one. What the hell's he doing, giving him a gun?
Good thing he loads him up with blanks, at least. God
knows what would happen if he made a mistake. That
would be it. He could get into real trouble. Horrible to think
about. We'd all be in for it then. You were wetting
yourselves I bet, eh . . .

LYOVCHIK (*brushing himself down*). S'pose . . .

CLERK. How about you, girl?

POPPET *doesn't answer. She is crouching on the edge of
the bench, holding her stomach with both hands.*

Course, you've got a little'un as well. Shouldn't get
stressed. I remember, when I was pregnant with Varka, I was
living with a right lad. Criminal type, covered in bloody
tattoos he was. He was chasing after me. Oh, he was. When
he was sober he was fairly quiet, wanted to settle down he
kept saying, tired of roaming . . . but a bit of the hard stuff
and he went off his head. Once he shouts out he wants some
fun and pokes me with a knife, just here. (*She points.*) Not
a real deep cut, of course – just a scratch. But all the same
it was horrible. And I was really young then, as well. Didn't
see them coming, as they say. I was really scared of him
after that. And now I wonder if Varka isn't so ugly because
all that deformed her. All that 'ecoli-gy' business was alright

back then. Course, she was hideous as a kid. I used to be embarrassed going to the children's hospital with her. Little babies are supposed to be all cute, and there she was looking like a piglet. God above, she looked like a piglet. And even now I'm not sure who she takes after. There isn't an animal like her on the planet, probably.

LYOVCHIK. He lost his marbles, has he?

CLERK. Who? My fellow?

LYOVCHIK. No. The bloke just now.

CLERK. Well, who the hell knows. He seems harmless enough. Sells the Communist paper on the local trains. Stands around with a banner at the demonstrations . . . 'Proletarians of the World Unite . . . ' Seen it myself. But as soon as he's had a few he starts acting up. He doesn't drink on his own, but he will if someone gives him a few. It's the second time that the useless sod has shot at me. First time was when I started selling vodka. He arrives first. Sober. Well that's it. He starts agitating to get me to shut up shop. Keeps me standing around while he gives a lecture. He got to me so much in the end that I gave him a blasting and threw him out. So what does the bastard do? Gets tanked up somewhere, takes his brother's gun and pokes it through the ticket window and gives it to me from two barrels. I was desperate for the toilet when it happened and so I shat myself. (*She laughs.*) I thought that was it and he'd killed me. Auntie Lusya Litvinenko is dead. I didn't know then that Fedya always loads it with blanks for him. He shot at Petrovna once. As an anti-social element or something. She had her head screwed on though and took his popgun off him, and then she made Fedya pay a ransom. Yeah . . . Maybe I shouldn't have slapped him. Hope I haven't disturbed things.

LYOVCHIK. He needs help.

CLERK. Who needs the hassle? Who's going to bother, eh? If he puts a hole in someone, then they will. But otherwise . . . (*She looks at* POPPET.) You've gone pale, love. Are you alright? Not feeling too good, eh?

POPPET *shakes her head.*

Mind yourself then. I've got some salts you can have.

POPPET. You don't ... Do you know? It's all wet down there ...

CLERK. What?

POPPET. All wet down there ...

CLERK (*comes over*). Let's have a look ...

POPPET (*presses her legs together*). What for?

CLERK. Come on then ... What you being like a little schoolgirl for? You're a grown woman. (*She looks.*) It's your waters, love.

POPPET. Y'what?

CLERK. Your waters have broken.

POPPET. What for?

CLERK. Well. Going to have a baby, aren't you?

POPPET. I don't want to. We've got more stuff to sell. I don't want to ...

CLERK. Well no one asked you. You're giving birth and that's it.

LYOVCHIK. But how come? It's too early.

CLERK. How many months?

POPPET. Eight.

CLERK. That's it then. Why did you decide to come to the middle of nowhere just when you were due?

LYOVCHIK. But people have babies after nine months ...

CLERK. Who told you that?

LYOVCHIK. That's how it's always been. Says in books.

CLERK. Things are written on fences and all ... You look like intelligent people and you go round believing what you read in books. Well, look at you two! So what are we going to do with you? A nice mess. People give birth at nine months . . . It's not like getting a passport. You give birth when you're ready to.

LYOVCHIK. Is the hospital far away?

POPPET (*stands up*). I'm not giving birth here.

CLERK (*sits her back down*). Sit down, girl. What sort of bloody hospital do you expect around here? Never even remotely been one. There was a first aid post once. But that went. But never ever a hospital. Around here people get on with it. At home. That's where they give birth and fall ill and end their days.

LYOVCHIK. How come?

CLERK. Like that. Simple. When you get back to your capital you can tell them how people live in Russia, 'cause they don't even have the faintest idea. Even if God was supposed to knock us out equal, we're only equal on the outside. Two arms, two legs and a head with a body. Every other way we're different. We're so different that it's frightening. Right. What are we going to do? And they want a hospital . . . Probably holding out for a private room as well. We'll have to make do. One of the men round here burnt himself really badly on the stove and his wife took him into town on the stopping train. He's sitting on the train and his skin's falling off him in great big bits. Passengers were going mad. Anyway the police decide to investigate at the station. Out with your papers, and all that. Course they didn't have anything with them – they hadn't exactly packed for the journey . . . So they took them in, started with the questions, phone calls. And this bloke, he hung on and hung on and then he went and died. Didn't even manage to tell them what he thought of them properly. So there you are. And you want hospitals on a plate. Arab sheiks or something, are you? Had it too good, you have.

POPPET. Lyovchik, tell her to eff off, will you?

CLERK. I'll tell you to eff off in a minute.

POPPET. Lyovchik . . .

CLERK. Keep your mouth shut!

POPPET. Shut yours, you old bitch!

CLERK. You say that again, eh . . .

POPPET. Lyovchik, let's get out of here . . .

CLERK. I'll give you 'get out' in a minute. I'm just about
ready to take off my boot and give you a hiding like I did
Mishanya. Then you'll 'get out of here' . . . You remember,
I'm running around worrying about you. But I couldn't give
a damn about your sort, it's the child I'm worried about. It's
not to blame is it? Even if its parents are miserable shits.

POPPET (*eyes filling with tears*). Lyovchik, tell her to go to . . .

LYOVCHIK. Where?

POPPET. Anywhere . . . Use the c-word . . .

LYOVCHIK. You fucking do it. You're really winding me up.

POPPET. Bastard. Don't you start as well.

LYOVCHIK. Go to . . . (*He moves away and sits down next to
the man. He rubs his face.*)

CLERK. Right. I'm off. I'll go and see Pashka Lavrenyova.
She's got five kids. An old hand. She'll take you. Look after
the office, will you. (*She goes.*) Bloody hell! Hospitals,
indeed . . . private room with a telly . . . (*She goes out.*)

Silence.

POPPET. Give us a fag.

LYOVCHIK. You've got them.

POPPET. Where? (*She rifles through her pockets.*) Which
pocket?

LYOVCHIK. How should I know, I'm not a mind reader.

POPPET. You're a bastard. That's what you are. (*She gets out
a cigarette and tries to light it but fails.*) Help me light up.

LYOVCHIK *gets up unwillingly and goes over to her and lights the cigarette. She takes his hand in a conciliatory way.*

What's wrong with you then?

LYOVCHIK (*still angry, but softening*). What you mean?

POPPET. Being like that.

LYOVCHIK. Like what?

POPPET. Like that.

LYOVCHIK (*takes back his hand*). Fucking good place to decide to have a baby.

POPPET. Like I did it on purpose . . .

LYOVCHIK (*mocking her*). 'Like I did it on purpose.' Couldn't you hang on or anything? Two more bloody days . . .

POPPET. Alright I won't then . . .

LYOVCHIK. Don't.

POPPET. Right. I won't. (*She gets up and throws away her cigarette.*) Let's go. (*She lifts the bags.*)

LYOVCHIK. Put them down.

POPPET. Right. I'm off. This place is pissing me off.

LYOVCHIK. I said, put them down.

POPPET. Let's go!

LYOVCHIK (*grabbing a bag*). Put them down . . . don't you get it?

POPPET. Let's go!

LYOVCHIK. Why are you being so bloody difficult. Sit down!

POPPET. Get off me! I'm going!

LYOVCHIK. Will you fucking well sit down! You're driving me mad!

POPPET. Get off me, you bastard! (*She tears away the bag.*)
Get off me, I said! Get off! Get off, you prick! I hate you,
you bastard! I hate you! (*She throws the bags across the
hall.*) Fuck off, you cunt! Get the fuck off! Fuck off! (*She
slaps him across the face.*) Fuck off . . . (*She sits down on
the floor and starts weeping.*) I wish you'd die . . . I
wouldn't even bury you, you animal. Do you understand?
You'll just lie there rotting . . . and the flies'll eat you . . .
Shit on you . . . You won't even see your bastard child . . .
I'll throw it under a train . . . myself . . . get it? D'you
understand?

LYOVCHIK *doesn't reply.*

Get it? I said, d'you understand me? Do you? WELL, DO
YOU? DO YOU? DO YOU?

*While she is talking the sound of an approaching train
grows louder. It comes closer and closer, roars louder and
louder.* POPPET *shrieks and shrieks . . . The train comes
closer and closer . . . At last everything is combined into a
horrible metallic gnashing, as if rusty cogs the size of the
universe were turning. The old drunk wakes up and gets up
from his place. He looks at* POPPET *and* LYOVCHIK *with
an understanding glance. He has tears in his eyes. The tears
roll down his cheeks and fall on the floor. And keep on
falling . . .*

End of Act One.

ACT TWO

Ten days have passed. It is early morning. The same station. The same benches, the same left-luggage lockers, the same pyramid of firewood by the stove. Everything is exactly as before. The only things that are missing are the drunk and the sign reading 'All gone'. Instead there is a board reading 'Closed temporarily' and the ticket window has a heavy greasy blind pulled over it.

LYOVCHIK, POPPET *and a woman, aged around fifty, enter the room.* LYOVCHIK *pushes in a pram. The pram is antediluvian and well-used.* POPPET *is not made-up. She has black rings under her eyes. She is holding a half-empty checked bag. The woman is also holding a bag.*

LYOVCHIK (*looks at his watch*). Plenty of time. Almost another whole hour. (*To* POPPET.) Are you allowed to sit down?

WOMAN. Yes she is.

POPPET *nods.*

Sit down, Shura.

The woman puts her bag down next to her.

Milk. Mind you don't break the jar. I wrapped it in a towel. But still . . . If something happened . . . Why don't I wait with you . . .

POPPET. There's no need, Auntie Pasha. You go on.

AUNTIE PASHA. Well you know best.

LYOVCHIK. Who's the milk for? Don't you feed with these? (*He points at his chest.*)

POPPET. She won't feed from me. 'Cause I smoked . . . it's bitter, isn't it.

LYOVCHIK. Unbelievable. Has an effect, does it?

AUNTIE PASHA. And what did you think?

LYOVCHIK (*rocking the pram*). We didn't think at all . . .

AUNTIE PASHA. The nappies are all in there. Don't bother
drying them out, Shura. Throw them away. They're old
anyway. And when you get there you can buy some. Have
you forgotten anything? (*She rifles through the bag. Pause.*)
Looks like you've got it all. I put some food in for you.
Don't forget about it or it'll go off.

POPPET. You shouldn't have. We could have bought some.

AUNTIE PASHA. Whatever next! Wasting your money. You'll
be needing every penny soon. Kids don't seem to eat much,
but the money you'll get through – just count it and it's
gone. I've brought up five myself, thank the Lord, and
I know.

LYOVCHIK. No need to go and frighten us.

AUNTIE PASHA. Frighten you . . . I'm just telling it like it
is. They're not goats, kids – you can't just send them off
to graze. You need a lot of time and energy for them.
Sometimes you think to yourself, what did I do that for,
sometimes you stop loving them . . . when you've had it.
But then it all passes, passes quickly and you'll be happy
again. That's how it is. (*Pause.*) Well, Shura, let's say
goodbye then.

POPPET. Yeah.

AUNTIE PASHA. By the way . . . make sure that the bubbles
don't fill the teat when you're feeding. She'll start playing
up. And for now don't wash her when she messes. Wet
some cotton wool and clean her with that. Do they boil
water on the train?

POPPET (*Nods.*) Uh-huh.

AUNTIE PASHA. Good. That's the best. Remember to test it
with your hand and wipe it dry.

POPPET. Right.

Pause.

AUNTIE PASHA. Not forgotten anything then. (*She reaches into the bag.*)

POPPET. You checked, Auntie Pasha.

AUNTIE PASHA. Did I? Never mind, I'll check again. (*She rummages in the bag. Pause.*) Everything's there. I didn't put in the goat's milk. She hasn't taken to it. The smell, I expect. This is cow's milk. It's a good cow, don't worry about it. The main thing is not to smash the jar. Then you'd have problems. If something happens get a packet of milk at one of the stations. And just ask the attendant to boil it up for you . . . I should have put it in a tin. Maybe I've got time to run back? I should make it, I think . . .

POPPET. No need, Auntie Pasha.

AUNTIE PASHA. Well, I s'pose we should say goodbye then.

POPPET. Mmm.

AUNTIE PASHA. When you get back, maybe you'll drop me a line, so I don't worry, eh? We're hardly strangers now.

POPPET. Mmm.

LYOVCHIK. We'll send a telegram.

AUNTIE PASHA. Letter would be better. Warmer, somehow. And cheaper. And write what you decide to call her.

POPPET. OK, Auntie Pasha.

AUNTIE PASHA. Perhaps you'll invite me to the christening, if you decide to christen her.

LYOVCHIK. Course we will. And we'll buy you a ticket.

AUNTIE PASHA. I'd find a way myself, for something like that.

Pause.

So, what now? Oh yes, Shurochka, I wanted to say as well, you should express so you don't lose it. 'Cause maybe she'll take to it, who knows? Alright?

POPPET. Mmm.

AUNTIE PASHA. Well, that's it then. Shura . . . don't hold it against me that I shouted at you when I was doing the birth. Now I understand you were the way you were because you were new to it – but then I thought you were just trying it on. I thought you'd kill the kid with your trying it on. You were pushing her in and out like a lollipop. I was really worried. I've had five myself and helped out with as many, but I still can't get rid of the nerves. Maybe I'll never get used to it. Like death. Doesn't matter how many you see, it's still the same . . . So, Shura, don't hold it against me, alright?

POPPET. I've forgotten it already, Auntie Pasha.

AUNTIE PASHA. You're kidding. Lusya and I swore at you so much that I'm still embarrassed, even now. Where did it all come from? Probably in our blood, all those bad words. Well, never mind. (*She looks at* LYOVCHIK.) Takes after her Daddy, she does.

LYOVCHIK. What, really? (*He looks into the pram.*) You must be able to tell . . . I can't see anything yet.

AUNTIE PASHA. She does, oh, she does.

LYOVCHIK. Well, you would know.

Pause.

AUNTIE PASHA. Well then Shura, good luck to you. Have a good journey. Look after your daughter. See how it's turned out: born here and she'll live there. And not where she was born . . . You bring her back at some point, eh? Show her her birthplace. And don't forget us. We'll always be pleased to hear from you. (*She wipes away a tear.*) I'm old, I am, and I don't want to leave you. I've got used to you. You've become like my own. Like my daughter and my grand-daughter. In a minute I'll get on that train with you . . . Off

you go then, take her. After all . . . well, that's enough . . .
I'll be off . . . or I'll start crying properly. Goodbye Shura,
my girl. (*She bends over and hugs and kisses* POPPET.)

POPPET. Bye bye, Auntie Pasha . . .

AUNTIE PASHA. Right . . . enough . . . I'm off.

POPPET. Auntie Pash . . .

AUNTIE PASHA. What? What do you want, Shura?

POPPET. No, nothing . . .

AUNTIE PASHA. Oh, I thought you said . . . Right, I'm off.
(*She goes over to* LYOVCHIK *and shakes his hand.*)

LYOVCHIK. How much do I owe you?

AUNTIE PASHA. What?

LYOVCHIK (*reaches into his money belt for money*). How
much did you spend on her?

AUNTIE PASHA (*recoils*). Whatever next.

LYOVCHIK. No, really.

AUNTIE PASHA. Do you think I . . . Goodbye. (*She goes
towards the door.*) You might move her over here as it's a
bit close. Get some fresh air . . .

POPPET. Alright, Auntie Pasha.

AUNTIE PASHA *leaves.*

LYOVCHIK (*pushes the pram to the door and then goes over
to* POPPET, *laughing*). Chatty old lady.

POPPET. She's only coming up to fifty.

LYOVCHIK. Just lady then. Didn't she go on, though . . . Took
her time leaving. Thought nothing would get rid of her. I
can just imagine what you went through, ten days at hers.
Felt like shooting yourself probably.

POPPET. It was alright.

LYOVCHIK. Yeah, right. I would have killed myself.

POPPET. Well I wouldn't.

LYOVCHIK. You're making it up. D'you know what I bought you?

POPPET. What?

LYOVCHIK (*gets out a green packet*). Fags.

POPPET. I'm not allowed to.

LYOVCHIK. Why? She said you wouldn't be able to feed, anyway.

POPPET. Maybe I will be able to. Later.

LYOVCHIK. Fuck it, eh. Let it drink cow's milk – what's the difference?

POPPET. A big difference.

LYOVCHIK. Well be like that then. I'm not going to force you, am I? (*Puts the packet away.*)

Pause.

Fancy a Chupa?

POPPET. No.

LYOVCHIK. Why?

POPPET. I just don't want one.

LYOVCHIK. Go on, take it.

POPPET. I said I didn't want one.

LYOVCHIK. What you being like that for?

POPPET. Like what?

LYOVCHIK. All like that . . .

POPPET. Like what?

LYOVCHIK. I don't know. All uptight or something.

POPPET. I'm not . . .

LYOVCHIK. Like you've become a mother and so straightaway you're throwing your weight around. Because actually I've become a father, too – so I could start all that as well.

POPPET. I'm not throwing my weight around.

LYOVCHIK (*gets out a Chupa Chups*). Take the Chupa then.

POPPET. I don't want it.

LYOVCHIK. Well don't ask later. (*Unwraps the Chupa and sticks it in his mouth.*)

Silence.

LYOVCHIK *goes over to the ticket window and looks in.*

Where's what's-her-name? The brewer. Isn't it her shift or something?

POPPET. It's hers.

LYOVCHIK. Why isn't she here then?

POPPET. She's quit.

LYOVCHIK. Yeah, right. She wanted to sit it out till her pension here.

POPPET. Didn't work out.

LYOVCHIK. Why not?

POPPET. Someone got poisoned by her vodka.

LYOVCHIK. What? Completely?

POPPET. Completely.

LYOVCHIK. Fuck. Him, was it? The Commie with the gun?

POPPET. No.

LYOVCHIK. Who then? (*Pause.*) Where's that guy . . . Who was asleep . . . the one who bit you?

POPPET. He was the one who got poisoned.

LYOVCHIK. Unbelievable. Really? D'you know where I got rid of the rest of the goods?

POPPET. She buried him herself. Paid for it all.

LYOVCHIK. Good thing. That way no one ends up in jail . . . bought herself off. I reckon she'd have had to buy off the relatives as well.

POPPET. He didn't have any. They were all dead.

LYOVCHIK. She was lucky then. Hey, guess what – while you were here I went and got a new batch of stuff.

POPPET. He left a house here.

LYOVCHIK. . . . And guess what . . . Erm, so what?

POPPET. We could buy it. It'd be cheap.

LYOVCHIK. What the hell for?

POPPET. Well . . .

LYOVCHIK. What do you mean, 'well'?

POPPET. Well.

LYOVCHIK. Buy ourselves a little place in Magadan as well. Just in case, like. Own real estate right across the country.

POPPET. There's a sawmill here. We could renovate it . . .

LYOVCHIK. What is wrong with you, Poppet?

POPPET. What?

LYOVCHIK. Are you alright in the head? You gone funny . . . The things you come out with . . . Awful. I reckon you've lost it a bit. Have you?

POPPET. No.

LYOVCHIK. Watch yourself then. Have a smoke. (*He gets out the packet.*)

POPPET. I don't want to.

LYOVCHIK. For fuck's sake, take it. You're winding me up
with this not smoking. I can see you want to.

POPPET. I don't.

LYOVCHIK. You do. (*He gets out a cigarette and sticks it in
her mouth.*)

POPPET *doesn't resist.* LYOVCHIK *puts it between her
lips and lights it.*

Take a drag, go on. It's not lighting, fuck it. Have a drag . . .

POPPET (*spits out the cigarette*). I said I don't want it.

LYOVCHIK. Alright, keep your hair on . . .

POPPET. Honestly I don't want it, love.

LYOVCHIK. OK, OK, I'm not forcing you . . . Anyway, they
took the lot. Like, when I left here, yeah, I got out at some
place, worse than this, imagine . . . But more people there
and even a school. So anyway I went along to this school
and told them I could do a presentation there. Slipped the
headteacher a hundred. All hunky-dory. Loads of people
came along and they took the lot off me. So I got back on
the train and went off for another lot. A bit less this time,
'course. You weren't with me, were you. So not bad, eh.
I was happy. Covered the ticket price straightaway. You get
a great audience around these places. Wow. What an
audience. God, they're like kids. The money you can make
around here, it's unbelievable. Just keep hauling it in . . .
keep it coming . . . Collect it up . . . Making money . . .
Hey, did that old bloke really snuff it?

POPPET. What?

LYOVCHIK. I said, was that bloke really poisoned?

POPPET. Mmm.

LYOVCHIK. Maybe he died naturally. Maybe his time was up.

POPPET. Poisoned. The spirit was bad.

LYOVCHIK. Fuck, I'm sorry for the old girl. Lost her business.

POPPET. She wanted to hang herself.

LYOVCHIK. Come on . . .

POPPET. It's true. She hanged herself right here. It was almost over. They cut her down and she survived. Afterwards she kept on howling. Kept saying there's no point in living. I came over myself to talk her out of it.

LYOVCHIK. You?

POPPET. Me

LYOVCHIK. Well, Poppet, I can see you've been . . . enjoying yourself. So what did you say to her?

POPPET. Lots.

LYOVCHIK. Like what?

POPPET. Can't remember right now.

LYOVCHIK. Oh, come on. You remember. What did you say to her?

POPPET. I can't remember.

LYOVCHIK. Don't lie. I know what you said. (*He declaims.*) We are given but one life and we should live it so that afterwards we are not tormented by the aimlessly wasted years. Is that what you said?

POPPET. I can't remember.

LYOVCHIK. Poppet, you've gone out of your mind, I reckon . . . Christ . . . We'll have to take you along to the loony bin. The way you're talking. It isn't healthy.

POPPET. Nothing wrong with it.

LYOVCHIK. Well I can tell you how it looks from here. Anyway, we'll get back and take you for treatment. At the 'Three Fishermen' . . . will you come? We can have a ball all night. Back to civilisation.

POPPET. And what about here?

LYOVCHIK. What you on about?

POPPET. I told her that it was never too late to change your life.

LYOVCHIK (*not understanding*). Told who? That's enough of that crap, Poppet. It's scary talking to you. Hey, let's talk about the higher things in life, eh? D'you know how much money we've got?

POPPET. No.

LYOVCHIK. Three guesses.

POPPET. I don't know.

LYOVCHIK. Well name a figure. It's not hard.

POPPET. Hundred roubles.

LYOVCHIK. Oh come on . . . you're really pissing me off now. (*Walks around the room.*) Seven thousand dollars. Happy now?

POPPET. Happy.

LYOVCHIK. There you go, eh. And we'll make more. A load. A whole load. Fuck it, ten whole loads.

POPPET. What for?

LYOVCHIK. Eh?

POPPET. What for?

LYOVCHIK (*stops*). Have you got it in your head to really piss me off?

POPPET. No.

LYOVCHIK. Well sit still and shut up then.

POPPET. Alright.

LYOVCHIK. What do you mean, alright? What are you being so touchy about? I don't get it.

POPPET. I'm not . . .

LYOVCHIK (*mocking her*). I'm not . . . Well I am. What don't you like, eh? That I went travelling round all these holes like royalty while you were . . .

POPPET. Don't shout, you'll wake her.

LYOVCHIK. I'm not shouting. I won't wake her. Just don't get all funny with me, please. 'Cause two can play at that. I'll get so funny, that you'll fucking well end up staying here. Shit, sitting there, not interested in anything, doesn't want a Chupa, doesn't want a smoke . . . So what do you want, eh? Shall I get my arse out for you?

POPPET. Fuck off.

LYOVCHIK (*starts smiling*). Hey. Now I recognise you. Come oñ then, say something about the Hermitage . . .

POPPET (*also smiling, but trying to hide it. Biting her lower lip*). Well, the Hermitage . . .

LYOVCHIK (*suddenly roars with laughter*). Fuck, Poppet . . . Fuck it . . . you should have seen yourself just then . . . Face like the back end of a bus! (*He bends double laughing.*)

POPPET. Fuck off!

LYOVCHIK. . . . back end of a bus! (*Roars.*)

POPPET. Piss off.

Pause.

LYOVCHIK (*stops laughing*). Want a Chupa?

POPPET. Alright then.

LYOVCHIK. Orange flavour?

POPPET. Whatever.

LYOVCHIK. Have an orange one.

POPPET. Alright.

LYOVCHIK (*gets out the Chupa and unwraps it*). And that . . . chatty lady you lived with . . . did she have one of our toasters?

POPPET. Yeah.

LYOVCHIK. And?

POPPET. She has it standing out.

LYOVCHIK. Just standing there?

POPPET. Yeah.

LYOVCHIK. Right.

POPPET. She thought you bake bread in it. She stuck some dough in it and the element burnt out.

LYOVCHIK. Fucking aborigines. Gotta get back home. (*He looks at his watch.*) We'll get the post train as far as Chelyabinsk and then fuck it, we'll get a separate compartment. I hate those open carriages. Really gets on my tits – faces, faces, faces everywhere. Each one stupider than the next. Have a Chupa. (*He gives her a Chupa Chups.*)

POPPET *takes it and holds it in her hand.* LYOVCHIK *looks in the pram.*

Why didn't you tell me we needed to buy a pram? This is a nightmare. What a total embarrassment it'll be on the train. It's a tank. Tramps push their bottles around in prams like this. Where did it come from?

POPPET. Auntie Pasha got it from someone.

LYOVCHIK. Probably got syphilis living in it.

POPPET. We washed it.

LYOVCHIK. What's the point. Alright. I'll get out at one of the long stops and try and buy one.

POPPET. Lyova, love . . .

LYOVCHIK. What?

POPPET. I probably . . .

At this moment the baby starts crying. LYOVCHIK *goes over to the pram.*

LYOVCHIK. What d'you do?

POPPET. Rock it.

LYOVCHIK. D'you have to sing?

POPPET. No.

LYOVCHIK *rocks the pram. The baby stops crying.*

LYOVCHIK. Is that all?

POPPET. Expect so.

LYOVCHIK (*leaves the pram and goes over to* POPPET). What were you saying, I didn't understand?

POPPET *doesn't answer. She looks at the floor.*

Hey . . .

POPPET. Lyova, love, I don't think I'm going to go . . .

LYOVCHIK. What?

Pause.

POPPET. I don't want to go back there.

LYOVCHIK. I don't get it. Say that again.

POPPET (*louder*). I'm not going.

LYOVCHIK. You off your head or something?

POPPET. Maybe.

LYOVCHIK. Come off it. Stop going on like that.

POPPET. I'm not going on. I'm just not leaving, that's all . . .

LYOVCHIK. Stop it, eh? What did I do?

POPPET. It's not you. I'm just tired, Lyov.

LYOVCHIK. What you tired of? Lugging the bags around? Counting money? What are you tired of?

POPPET. Tired of being a bitch.

LYOVCHIK. Of being what?

POPPET (*gets up*). A bitch. One of many. 'Cause it's trendy to be a bitch there . . . Trendy to hate and look down on everyone. You look at them and feel bitter inside. They look at you and feel bitter inside. Everyone joins in . . . it's like we're doomed. Little boy comes up to you on the street and asks for bread and you tell him to fuck off. Even if something inside you wants to give him a few kopecks. But you tell him to fuck off. 'Cause no one else gives him any money, so why should you. Why should you, eh . . . So you tell him to fuck off. And then you make it up in your head that he earns more than you do . . . When he doesn't really earn anything at all . . .

LYOVCHIK. What little boy, what you . . .

POPPET. I don't want to be like that anymore. I want to be like a real person . . . like Auntie Pasha. Like them. That's how I want to be. You can be like shit to them, and they'll still be kind to you. And they'll even apologise for not giving you enough. That's how I want to be. And how I want my daughter to be. So I don't have to think what a bitch I am. So I don't have that pain. Do you understand that?

LYOVCHIK. Stop screaming, you nut.

POPPET (*quieter*). I'm not screaming.

LYOVCHIK. You are.

POPPET. I'm not screaming. But the main thing is that you see it all. You see that you're not living right. But you still carry on living like that. And then you even start enjoying it, and you get a kick from it, from being a bitch. And at that point your soul dies.

LYOVCHIK. And your arse? Does that die, too?

POPPET. Stop it.

LYOVCHIK. No you stop it. So you've seen the fucking light, have you? Found higher meaning?

POPPET. I have.

LYOVCHIK. You've just had it too good, you have. You want to stay here? Help yourself. Be my guest. Off you go. Go and live with the cows. Howl at the moon. You think there'll be tears, eh? Go to hell. No one will be shedding tears. No one needs you. You stay here. Let's see how you get on here. After ten days you reckon you're one of them. Yeah right. Enjoy. You'll be washing in a tub and shitting in a ditch for a month at most before you come crying . . . You think I don't know you?

POPPET. You don't.

LYOVCHIK. I do. I've got you down.

POPPET. No you haven't.

LYOVCHIK. Go on then. Stay. Like I care.

POPPET. And you could stay too.

LYOVCHIK. Me?

POPPET. You.

LYOVCHIK. You think I'm off my head, too. I don't reckon I've lost it yet.

POPPET. No I mean it.

LYOVCHIK. What do you mean, 'mean it'? You're off your head.

POPPET. There's a sawmill here. I told you.

LYOVCHIK. So what?

POPPET. We could rebuild it.

LYOVCHIK. And what? Walk around singing songs? La la la . . .

POPPET. We could sell the flat. And this money. That would be enough. I went and found out.

LYOVCHIK. You went and found out just like that?

POPPET. Yeah.

LYOVCHIK. Well then it's all arranged. I won't argue then, keep quiet.

POPPET. And the people would have work.

LYOVCHIK. Yeah, course. And wages. And meaning in their lives. All hunky-dory.

POPPET. And we could live alright.

LYOVCHIK. Wow, yeah, we'd be living the life. I can't argue. We'd build schools all over the place, circuses, fuck it, nursery schools . . . eh?

POPPET. I mean it.

LYOVCHIK. You think I'm joking? I mean it too. Your idea has inspired me.

POPPET. Lyova . . .

LYOVCHIK. What, 'Lyova'? Lyova is already planning how he's going to regenerate Russia. And how they're going to put up a monument to him for his work, made out of pure gold. After his death.

POPPET. Stop it.

LYOVCHIK. Hey, I've just got going. And then the grateful generations to come will read about Lyova – a little paragraph in their school history books. With pictures: 'Lyova taking the first step on the road to the regeneration of Russia: Selling his flat.' And here he is knocking the last nail into the rebuilt sawmill . . .

POPPET. Stop it.

LYOVCHIK. And here he is building the largest hydro-electric power station in the world on the local stream of sludge . . .

POPPET. I said, stop it!

LYOVCHIK. Alright, that's it then. Enough. (*He looks at his watch.*) The train will be here soon. Let's go out.

POPPET. I'm not going.

LYOVCHIK. Stop it now, eh? We can finish this on the train.

POPPET. There's nothing to finish. I'm not going.

LYOVCHIK. I said, cut it out. Enough. This will all be desert soon. Taiga. Forest.

POPPET. It's back there that there'll be desert. Everyone killing each other. Ripping each other apart.

LYOVCHIK. Why are you being so difficult?

POPPET. 'Cause I realised . . . when I was giving birth . . . and after, when . . .

LYOVCHIK. I'll give you a smack in a minute and then you'll realise. Come to your senses . . .

POPPET. When I gave birth . . . I saw God.

LYOVCHIK. No, really? And what did he look like? Have a beard, did he?

POPPET. No.

LYOVCHIK. Wasn't him then. God's got a beard. So what happened after that?

POPPET. What difference does it make?

LYOVCHIK. No go on, now you've started. I love tales about God. Me and him are old mates.

POPPET (*after a pause*). At the beginning he was standing in the corner looking at me all the time. He was whispering something . . .

LYOVCHIK. Praying was he? What else he got to do?

POPPET. And then he came over. He stroked my forehead. And kissed me . . .

LYOVCHIK. What a bastard! Kissing other men's wives, eh? Fucking Casanova.

POPPET (*starts to cry*). And then I understood that he hadn't left me. I betrayed him and abandoned him and he didn't betray me . . . and he'll never leave me. He'll always be with me. 'Cause he never leaves anyone. Never . . .

LYOVCHIK. Amazing guy, eh.

POPPET. And I told the ticket clerk, Auntie Lusya, about him and she believed me and she said she wouldn't do anything to herself. She said that she'd live. She'd live – that's what she said. Live. And I want to live, too. LIVE, Lyova.

LYOVCHIK. Go on then, live. Am I standing in your way? Live a hundred years if you like.

POPPET. You haven't understood.

LYOVCHIK. Alright. That's enough. Are you going?

POPPET. No.

LYOVCHIK. We're off then.

POPPET. We?

LYOVCHIK. Us. Who else? (*He nods at the pram.*) With her. Did you really think I'd leave her here? No way. It's not going to happen. I may be a bastard, but I'm not having my offspring scattered all over the place.

POPPET. I won't give her to you.

LYOVCHIK. What you say, darling?

POPPET. I won't give her to you. I gave birth to her.

LYOVCHIK. Yeah. And what came before that? Think about it?

POPPET. Nothing.

LYOVCHIK. Come off it! Have you conveniently forgotten how much I spent so you could have her? Eh? Remember that? How many abortions you had when you were screwing around. Eh? That's how I remember it . . . But now you're a fucking saint, eh? Seen the light and visions of God.

POPPET. I'll give you the money back.

LYOVCHIK. Give it back then.

POPPET. I'll pay you back.

LYOVCHIK. I need it now. Come on.

POPPET. You've got it. My money's in there, too.

LYOVCHIK. Yeah? How much?

POPPET. I don't know.

LYOVCHIK. Yeah, well there's nothing there, 'cause you haven't got any. You spent all yours. You think I bought you all those clothes with my own money. Fuck off, kid.

POPPET. I'll give it back to you later.

LYOVCHIK. I'm not arguing am I? You pay me back and you can take her.

POPPET. Lyova, you're joking, aren't you . . .

LYOVCHIK. Course I'm joking. I'm the fucking funny man.

POPPET. You're joking . . .

LYOVCHIK. Joking. Ha. Ha. So how many abortions did you have, little girl? Don't you remember then? D'you know, you've got a little card . . . from the clinic. And there's a box on it labelled abortions. And in the box there's a number. Do you know what it is? Double figures. That's how it is. Twelve or fifteen. Remember that? And now you're the fucking saint. Everyone's a bitch and she's a saint. Bugger you. You can fuck off. God doesn't come to people like you. He keeps as far away as he can. And how many blokes did you screw? You can't remember? Hundred? Five hundred? A million? Why is it you didn't see God each time you got laid by one of them? Eh? And when you had your bastards fed to a vacuum cleaner. Eh?

Pause.

So what'll it be? Give us the money or we're off.

POPPET. I hate you.

LYOVCHIK. It's mutual.

POPPET. I HATE YOU.

LYOVCHIK. I KNOW. YOU SAID.

POPPET. I hate you!

LYOVCHIK. Shut up. Let's have the money or we're off.
What's it going to be? You haven't got any money. Right.
Bye then.

*He takes the checked bag, goes over to the pram and wheels
it to the door.*

POPPET. Don't touch it, you bastard! (*She runs over and
grabs the pram.*)

LYOVCHIK. What's fucking wrong with you? Let go!

POPPET. You said you were joking, Lyova . . .

LYOVCHIK. Who? Me?

POPPET. You were joking. You don't need her.

LYOVCHIK. I do.

POPPET. You'll turn her into a bitch.

LYOVCHIK. So what?

POPPET. She'll only want clothes and money.

LYOVCHIK. So what? Not bad. Nice. That's how I want her to
be . . .

POPPET. Lyova, please!

LYOVCHIK. What's wrong, little girl?

POPPET. Let us go, Lyovochka.

LYOVCHIK. Pay. Everything costs money now.

POPPET. I'll give it back later.

LYOVCHIK. You going to rebuild the sawmill, yeah?

POPPET. I'll find . . .

LYOVCHIK. I've had about as much as I can fucking take. Get your hands off.

POPPET. I'll find . . .

LYOVCHIK. Get your hands off, you schiz!

POPPET. No I won't.

LYOVCHIK (*looks at his watch*). What are you on? The train will be here any minute.

POPPET. I'm not letting you go.

LYOVCHIK. Right, that's enough. Come over here. (*He goes over to the ticket window*). I want to say something to you . . .

POPPET (*follows him*). I won't let you go whatever.

LYOVCHIK. OK, so you won't let us go . . . (*He stops.*)

POPPET (*goes up to him*). Say it then.

LYOVCHIK. Look at this (*He points to something on the wall.*)

POPPET *looks.* LYOVCHIK *smashes her in the stomach with his fist.* POPPET's *face changes. She steps back, panting, then she crouches and lays down on the ground.*

LYOVCHIK (*shouting, but quietly*). You've pissed me off once and for all, you bitch! Get it? I'm sick to death of your fucking trouble-making. You're a bitch from hell. You can die down there for all I care! Die! And the flies will be all over you! Eating you! And shitting on you and not on ME! Understand? Thinks she's a fucking crystal vase! Thumbelina or something! You're a slut out of the gutter! Thinks God came to her! Kissed her! He didn't kiss you, he fucked you! Fucked you in your every hole like the scum you are! Like the cheapest whore! Understand?

Understand? Right. That's enough. (*He looks at his watch.*)
We're off. Bye then. (*He bends down and whispers almost
inaudibly.*) Fuck off. Fuck off. Fuck off . . .

*He goes to the door and opens it. Then he rolls out the
pram and goes out.*

POPPET (*turns over and looks at the door, crying or maybe
whispering*). I hate you! I hate you! I hate you all! All of
you, you Bastards! Bitches! Bastards! Disgusting bitches!
You'll burn in hell! In hell! You'll go to hell! You will!
Bitches! You animals! Vermin! You'll burn in hell! All of
you! You left him! Betrayed him! Traitors! Traitorous
bastards! You'll all burn in hell! I hate you!

*The baby starts crying outside. Its wails are terrifying, not
like a child's crying.*

POPPET *puts her hands over her ears. She sits down and
shouts up at the ceiling.*

God, give me strength! Give me strength, God. Give me
strength, Father! I love you, Father! I love you! I love you!
I love you! Give me strength. Father . . . Father . . . My
Father!

The sound of the train approaching. It sounds its horn.
POPPET *looks at the door for one second and then stares
back at the ceiling. She shouts out.*

I hate you! You can fuck off! Fucking well fuck off! I don't
need you! I'm not your daughter! You're nothing to me! I
don't want you! You're the bastard! You, not me!!

Understand? Do you understand!!! UNDERSTAND!!!

*The train flies into the station. The sound of a horn, every-
thing shakes and vibrates. Plaster breaks off and drops
down from the ceiling. It falls in* POPPET's *eyes. The bag
rolls across the seat and onto the floor. There is the sound
of breaking glass. White milk, as white as snow, spreads
across the floor. It spreads and mixes with the dust on the
floor and becomes blacker and blacker . . . blacker and
blacker. At last the train stops and everything quietens.*

Silence. POPPET *stands up. She wipes the plaster out of her eyes.* LYOVCHIK *runs in.*

LYOVCHIK. Well, get a fucking move on. The pram's already in the train. It's just about to leave.

POPPET. I'm coming. Can't you see, got something in my eyes.

LYOVCHIK. Get a move on . . .

POPPET. I'm coming. Stop getting at me. Give us a fag.

LYOVCHIK. You can smoke on the train.

POPPET. You scrooge.

LYOVCHIK. Fuck's sake, there you go then. (*He gives her the packet.*)

They go out. All that is left is the black puddle on the floor. But in it the sky, and not the ceiling, is reflected. The night sky. The moon is there. The planets and stars. Lots of stars. Millions. Billions. All the universe is reflected in this puddle. And the stars are flickering in it. Shining. Alight.

And the milk is suddenly no longer black, but white. White, like milk. White, like snow.

Darkness.

The End.

A Nick Hern Book

Black Milk first published in Great Britain in 2003
as an original paperback by Nick Hern Books Limited,
14 Larden Road, London W3 7ST in association with
the Royal Court Theatre, London

Typeset by Country Setting, Kingsdown, Kent CT14 8ES

Printed and bound in Great Britain by Bookmarque,
Croydon, Surrey

A CIP catalogue record for this book is available from
the British Library

ISBN 185459 730 2